Prepare for War

**RANDALL J.
BREWER**

PREPARE FOR WAR

CONTENTS

INTRODUCTION

The call to battle is as old as time itself. From the earliest chapters of Scripture, we witness the Lord raising up men to confront enemies, defend the weak, and advance His Kingdom. Joel 3:9-10 resounds with urgency, "Proclaim this among the nations: Prepare for war! Wake up the mighty men, let all the men of war draw near, let them come up." These words are not an abstract idea or a suggestion for the faint of heart. They are a clarion call for every man who bears the name of Christ. The command is clear: it is time to rise. It is time to awaken the warrior within. It is time to fulfill the sacred role God has assigned.

Throughout history, God has called men to stand in the gap. Consider Moses, standing resolute before Pharaoh, not with the sword of man but with the authority of God. Recall David, a shepherd boy armed only with a sling and faith, defeating Goliath and shaping the destiny of Israel. Remember the early apostles, facing imprisonment, persecution, and death, yet advancing the Kingdom of God with courage and conviction. These men understood a profound truth: the battle is real, the stakes are eternal, and God equips those He calls.

Today, the enemy has not disappeared. His tactics have changed, but his mission remains the same: to destroy faith, to weaken men, and to silence the voices of righteousness. The battle may not always be fought on a visible battlefield, but it rages in homes, workplaces, churches, and within the hearts of men. Temptation, fear, apathy, and doubt are weapons of the enemy - subtle, insidious, and relentless. A man who refuses to prepare, to stand, and to fight will be overpowered by forces he cannot see yet cannot ignore.

Being a warrior for God is not about physical prowess, military skill, or personal ambition. It is about spiritual strength, moral courage, and unyielding faith. It is about embracing discipline, nurturing character, and committing to a life of obedience. The true warrior understands that prayer is a weapon, Scripture is a shield, and God's power is the ultimate source of victory. The warrior stands firm, not because he is unshakable, but because his foundation rests upon the Rock of Ages.

This book is designed to awaken that warrior in you. It is written for the man who feels the stirrings of purpose in his heart, for the one who longs to step fully into the role God intended, and for every son of God who desires to rise to the challenge of spiritual warfare. You will discover principles rooted in the Word of God, illustrated through history, and applied to modern life. You will be called to assess your strengths, confront your weaknesses, and rise above complacency.

"Prepare For War" will teach you to stand with courage, to fight with wisdom, and to advance with clarity of purpose. It will challenge you to lead, to protect, and to inspire those around you. It will remind you that victory is not achieved by chance, but by preparation, by perseverance, and by unwavering commitment to the call of God.

Men of God, the time for hesitation is over. The nations rage, darkness advances, and the enemy waits to exploit the unprepared. Yet the God of heaven calls you to rise, to stand, and to fight. This is your moment. This is your calling. Will you answer? Will you embrace the mantle of a warrior for the Kingdom of God? The battle is real. The call is urgent. The time is now. Prepare for war!

| 1 |

"THE WARRIOR SPIRIT"

The book of Revelation tells of the war of Satan against God, against the Lamb of God and the saints of God. It is a battle between good and evil, right and wrong, light and darkness. The battle between righteousness and unrighteousness is an eternal struggle that began in the Garden of Eden. We read of Satan's attack on Job and his temptation of Jesus in the wilderness. It was the devil who worked among the heathen nations who brought about terrorist attacks against Israel. It was he who influenced the minds of the religious leaders to crucify Christ. Jesus called the devil your enemy in Matt. 13:39 and 1 Peter 5:8 says, "Your adversary the devil walks about like a roaring lion seeking whom he may devour." 1 John 3:8 says the devil prompts people to sin so they'll become like him. Paul spoke of the wiles of the devil describing him as crafty, clever, and cunning (Eph. 6:11).

The devil is evil and he fills the world with wickedness. He is a liar and a murderer and he spreads envy, jealousy, and hate. He has seduced the hearts of many. The devil divides families, churches, and nations. He invades our homes with filthy entertainment and fills our minds with lustful thoughts. He calls good, evil, and evil, good. He destroys the sanctity of human life. He glorifies perversion and undermines godly values. He attacks Christianity and desires most of all to destroy you. He is the venomous serpent and the dangerous dragon. He has declared war on the body of Christ and now is the time to declare war on him, time to fight for what's dear to us. 1 Tim. 1:18 (CSB) says, "Timothy, my son, I am giving you this instruction in keeping with the prophecies previously made about you, so that you may strongly engage in battle."

If you want to be a real man of God, know with certainty that God won't take you to the playground, He'll take you to the battleground. Forget the idea that becoming a real man is like a walk in the park. Make no mistake about it, there will be times of struggle, deprivation, and sacrifice. The day you stood up and declared that you will be a true man of God, is the day the devil declared war on you. For sure, anyone who chooses to be on the side of the Lord Jesus Christ will face severe opposition from Satan and his followers. This is war and the devil will do everything he can to destroy your life The home you live in and the church you attend is under attack and it's time for you to declare war. This is not fictional but a very real war in which not everyone comes out as more than a conqueror. Paul warns that some will be "shipwrecked" (1 Tim. 1:19) because they didn't put on the whole armor of God and were not able to withstand the devil's attacks on the evil day.

It is sad but true that most men in the church are weak-kneed Christians. They don't fight for their marriage, their children, their church, their freedom and liberties. On the contrary, all men have been commanded by God to fight! We have been charged to declare war! This is not a video game and in the game of life there are no second chances. We are all in a war and the question is are we going to advance, or are we going to retreat? Are we going to gain ground, or lose ground? In this battle, you cannot be a pacifist or you'll die where you stand. Never walk around with your head held down beaten and abused. No, stand strong with your hearts on fire with determination to take back what the enemy has stolen. Never forget the power and authority you carry as a man of God. Be bold and unwavering in the face of challenges and fears. Have an attitude of victory when facing difficult situations.

In order to prepare for war, you must first accept the reality of war. There is a tremendous war raging around us in the spiritual realm and each of us are involved and affected by this war. The road to authentic manhood is difficult and many battles will have to be fought and won. Even though we cannot see it, this war has greater significance than any war fought on earth since the beginning of time.

Ever since the Garden of Eden the devil has been committed to destroying everything God has done. How much more abuse will you take from him before you stand up and say, "Enough is enough!" The incomprehensible horror and suffering inflicted by physical wars ends at death while the impact and consequences of spiritual wars are eternal. The results of not fighting are devastating. Don't let financial success, good health, and a general state of well-being fool you into thinking you are not in a war. For sure, the battle for your manhood is an ongoing war and you can never let your guard down.

All of God's men are called to be warriors. You can't play games with the devil. He declared war on the church thousands of years ago and most men have not declared war on him. Know this, when the men of God do nothing, evil prevails. This is why now is the time for war. Enough is enough. No more will the devil be allowed to steal, kill, and destroy (John 10:10). The good news is that God strengthens His people for war. You don't have to rely on your own strength when you understand that God is on the side of the righteous. Whatever God calls you to do, he'll give you all you need to accomplish it. 2 Sam. 22:35 says, "He teaches my hands to make war so that my arms can bend a bow of bronze." And when you fight, God will be right there fighting with you. Deut. 1:30, "The Lord your God, who goes before you, He will fight for you, according to all He did for you in Egypt before your eyes."

Speaking of the devil, Rev. 12:11 says, "They overcame him by the blood of the Lamb and by the word of their testimony." You can't overcome the enemy without a fight. If God completely smoothed the way for us, what would there be to overcome? If God made everything easy, how would He test our loyalty? How would we be prepared to work in His kingdom? Sometimes it's good to fight, especially if there is something worth fighting for. On more than one occasion in the Bible the Christian life is compared to a conflict on a battlefield. For example,

1 Tim. 6:12 says, "Fight the good fight of faith, lay hold on eternal life, to which you were also called." 2 Tim. 2:3 says, "You therefore must endure hardship as a good soldier of Jesus Christ." Paul goes on to say in 2 Tim. 4:7, "I have fought the good fight, I have finished the race, I have kept the faith." Men today are under attack like never before and this is why you need to stand up and fight.

Refuse to walk in fear. Prov. 28:1 says, "The wicked flee when no one pursues, but the righteous are bold as a lion." Boldness is a spiritual strength, a mark of spiritual empowerment. Boldness is granted in response to prayer amidst persecution (Acts 3:41). Ps. 138:3 says, "In the day when I cried out, You answered me, and made me bold with strength in my soul." Men of integrity need to wake up and take a stand for the Word of God. Rom. 13:11 says, "It is time for us to wake up! For our full salvation is nearer now than when we first believed." In other words, time is running out and Christian motives are meant to incite moral duties. It is time to wake up out of our slumber and discern the times we are living in. This, in turn, should lead us to action. Joel 3:9 says, "Prepare for war! Wake up the mighty men, let all the men of war draw near, let them come up."

Living as a true man of God is not an easy life. If you are serious about glorifying God with your manhood, then prepare for war because you will have a fight on your hands. The end is near and you must start doing those things that need to be done. Wake up! Take off your night clothes and put on clothes appropriate for the work God is calling you to do. Never are you to stop offering your body to God as a living and holy sacrifice acceptable to Him (Rom. 12:1). When the call for war goes forth be the first person to say, "Here I am! Send me" (Is. 6:8). Now is the time for war. Time is running out, opportunities are fleeting, life is short. The time to obey God and go to war is now! There is no time for apathy, complacency, or indifference. John MacArthur said, "Wisdom numbers the days, sees the limited time, and buys the opportunity. Shun opportunities for evil and seize opportunities for good."

No real man should be asleep, in a drowsy state of spirituality. Martin Luther once said, "Awake! Awake! Hear the call of the Lord while we still have light to work!" Now is the time to wake up, to throw off the hypnotic state the world has put you in. Too many men are walking in their sleep doing nothing more than going through the motions. These are the men who go to church meetings and bow their heads when prayers are said. They read the Bible once in a while but pay no attention to what it says. They're inwardly asleep. Wake up and live with a sense of urgency. Rest assured, the devil isn't sleeping in his quest to take you down. Stop being a passive, uninvolved, indifferent Christian. There is a call going out to all sleeping men to wake up! Stop going through the motions of obedience without any real heart involvement and with a lack of enthusiasm.

It is time for war and this means you must remain intense in your desire to please God. With all your heart commit yourself totally to love what God loves and hate what God hates. Fight on! Spend and be spent (2 Cor. 12:15). Never settle for a casual religious experience. To go to war you must give your whole heart, mind, and strength to the task. You will accomplish much for the Lord if you don't fall asleep on the job. Act purposefully and intelligently. Fulfill your destiny with strength, boldness, and courage. Jesus said in Matt. 11:12, "The kingdom of God suffers violence, and the violent take it by force." Get fed up! Get violent! Draw a line in the sand and tell the devil, "Enough is enough!" You won't get anywhere and you won't do anything worthwhile or accomplish anything of significance until you get fed up with the wiles of the devil and do something about it.

You can wish, hope, and cry all day long but nothing will happen until you get fed up. For sure, things will start happening when a holy fervor rises up on the inside of you. Your countenance will change, you'll speak with authority, and you'll walk in dominion. Get aggressive and stirred up once again for what rightfully belongs to you. Get fed up with going without and then rise up and exercise your God-given authority over the devil. Live by the sword and never back off. The victory is yours if you get fed up and never give up. War has been declared and you can't have a lukewarm attitude when it comes to fighting the enemy. Don't be a weak-kneed nobody but rise up and go to war for the glory of God. Don't be afraid of the devil for he was defeated at the cross. Instead, make him be afraid of you. Rise up for you are a warrior in the army of the Lord by choice and by command.

Living as a true man of God is not an easy life. If you are serious about glorifying God with your manhood, then prepare for war because you will have a fight on your hands. All men have the warrior spirit inside of them. Warriors are always ready to go to war and fight for what is right. They fight with everything that is inside of them. The warrior spirit gives them the determination to take on any challenge. It gives them the desire to win at all costs. It is a divine honor for warriors to fight for what is right. The warrior says, "I have a clear goal. I have a clear mission. I have a meaningful purpose." Warriors are certain about the direction they're going in life. They know they are on the right path. The warrior says, "I can, I will, I must!" There is zero hesitation in the heart of a warrior. The warrior says, "I will not back down. I will not yield. I will fight until my last breath and do everything to win."

The warrior says, "I am ready. I will act now. I will fight with everything I have inside me. I will not be defeated." The warrior will fight for what is right no matter the odds, no matter what the potential consequences may be. The warrior says, "It is not over until I say it is over!' Warriors decide what they want in life and never back down until they get it. They pave their own path and walk in the direction they know to be right. They know they can handle whatever challenges life throws at them. They know God would not give them challenges they could not handle. Warriors are strong in the Lord and in the power of His might (Eph. 6:10). Warriors will die before they give up. They are committed to the goal and will not stray from it no matter what. You are a warrior! Warriors do not back down! Warriors never quit! Warriors fear nothing! Pick up your sword and stand tall in the confidence God has given you. Stand strong in your faith. Know what you want. Focus on it. Work for it. Being a warrior is what manhood is all about.

To be a victorious overcomer is going to take loyalty, courage, self-denial, vision, understanding, and a whole lot of sacrifice. When the enemy attacks resist him, hold your ground and go on the offensive. To cower before the devil is to invite sure defeat. The Bible says the timid man falls into a thousand snares (Prov. 29:25). The only way to obtain victory is to stand up and go to war. When you're clothed with the garment of a righteous lifestyle and strengthened in the inner man you will be most effective in your resistance against the devil's diabolical attacks. 1 Peter 5:9 says, "Resist him, standing firm in the faith." Stand up to the devil. Take a firm stand against him and never back down. Instead of being afraid of the devil, make him be afraid of you. The Greek word for "resist" is "anthistemi" and is a picture of a face-to-face confrontation. It involves not only a psychological attitude but also a corresponding behavior.

The term "standing firm" means 'to be unmovable in the face of opposition.' Do not surrender! Do not give up any ground! Do not back down! Move forward with all you've got! Even those not yet strong can resist the devil if they choose to. Charles Simeon said, "Satan is not only checked but terrified, and vanquished, by the resistance of the weakest Christian." This means there is no excuse for not resisting the devil. He is no match for even those recently saved believers. All it takes is one word of resistance and he will surely flee. By depending on the Lord even the weakest Christian can cause the devil to tremble in his boots. The truth is the devil is not all powerful as some make him out to be. 1 John 2:14 (AMP) says, "I write to you, young men, because you are strong and vigorous, and the Word of God is already abiding in you, and you have been victorious over the wicked one."

War cannot be avoided. We cannot remain neutral. In one sense, we really have no choice. We either fight or we die. Standing firm in faith is the solid foundation from which to fight this war. There needs to be a battle cry going forth in the world today. It must originate in the hearts of men who fear God and it must be sounded aloud. We are living in desperate times. Time is short and our days are numbered. Sin is ever increasing. What was unheard of 50 years ago is common and the norm in today's society. Lawlessness and idolatry abound. Character and ethics are a thing of the past. Men in the church have been silent for too long. Now is the time to stand up and sound the alarm. We need to prepare for war and man the battle stations. We need to live out what it says in Prov. 28:1, "The righteous are bold as a lion." Men need to find their voice in this wayward society. It's time to rise up and take a stand like never before. It's time to prepare for war!

We are in a spiritual war. This war is not fought in the deserts and jungles and oceans. This war takes place in a dimension we cannot see, and it's fought with weapons that are not of this world. We wage war in the heavenlies, tearing down principalities and everything that exalts itself against the power and knowledge of God (2 Cor. 10:5). We fight a spiritual war with spiritual weapons against a spiritual enemy. Make no mistake about it, the devil wants to lead you into greater levels of darkness. He wants to make you behave like him so you can help carry out his evil work on the earth. He wants to control you without you knowing it. He wants to snare you and bind you and steal your testimony. His primary goal is to render the Christian man ineffective in the kingdom of God. He wants to put you in a state of retreat rather than a forward march. Stop letting the enemy lull you to sleep. Wake up and act like a man. The devil has declared war on you; it's time for you to declare war on him!

| 2 |

"KNOW YOUR ENEMY"

It cannot be denied that spiritual conflict is inevitable. You are going to face a spiritual battle if you are a believer of Jesus Christ. However, you don't have to be defeated by the enemy. Eph. 6:10,11 says, "Finally, be strong in the Lord and in the power of His might. Put on the whole armor of God that you may be able to stand against the schemes of the devil." If you read the last page of the Bible you'll learn that it doesn't end well for the devil. Until then he'll forever try to convince you not to worship God, that you can be your own god. Satan got kicked out of heaven and fell to the earth like lightning (Luke 10:18). You live on the earth and this means you occupy the same geographical territory as the devil and his angels. What is he doing right now on the earth? The same thing that got him kicked out of heaven. He is leading a rebellion against God and he is trying to influence you to join him.

Make no mistake about it, Satan is alive and well on planet Earth. He is here to destroy you and your family. Sad to say, more times than not he is successful because we stand by and let it happen. We've become passive like Adam who stood next to Eve and did nothing as she was deceived into eating the fruit of the tree on the knowledge of good and evil. Instead of being passive, 1 Peter 5:8 says, "Be alert and of sober mind. Your enemy the devil prowls around like a roaring lion looking for someone to devour." Lions on the plains of Africa look for prey who are weak and vulnerable to their attack. They look for prey who aren't paying attention. Their heads are in the grass eating and they don't look up. The lion is vigilantly watching to see which animal will be his next meal. He's watching to see which animal's mind is clouded, thinking too much about eating instead of its own survival.

Peter identifies who the enemy is and gives us instructions on how to deal with him. The first thing we're told to do is be alert. This means to wake up and pay attention. You need to be aware of your surroundings and not be caught off guard. 1 Thess. 5:6 says, "So then let us not sleep as others do but let us be alert and sober." You must be forever watchful and ready to respond to the attacks of the enemy when they come. You know they're coming so there is no excuse not to be prepared when they do come. Being alert and vigilant is like carefully crossing a river while stepping on slippery stones. If you don't pay strict attention to what you're doing, you could end up in the water. With a sense of urgency you must stay awake and be alert at all times. In spiritual warfare you can't be lazy and let your guard down lest you become victims of the enemy.

Being alert is required because the enemy never shows himself for who he is. He disguises himself as an angel of light and his servants disguise themselves as servants of righteousness (2 Cor. 11:14,15). To take a stand against the enemy you must be sober-minded. You can't be clouded in your mindset and in your judgments. Your thinking must be self-controlled and well-balanced at all times. It is your duty to remain sober and watchful. You must always show sound, moral judgment. You must be clear-headed and free from any form of mental and spiritual intoxications. The Greek word "nepho" describes a condition free from every form of mental and spiritual loss of self-control. It is a picture of a calm, steady state of mind that evaluates things correctly. Always be alert so you can guard against the enemy's attacks. Being sober minded enables you to see things without the distortions caused be fear, worry, and doubt.

Long ago the ancient Chinese military strategist Sun Tzu said in his book "The Art Of War' that the first rule of warfare is to know your enemy. To prepare for war, you must know who your enemy is. Always be aware that the devil will do all he can to trip you up and get you to fall. Daily he plots against you to take you down. He prowls around looking for someone to devour. He can't devour everybody. That's why he's looking for somebody to devour. A bully knows who to mess with, and he knows who to leave alone. Your spouse is not your enemy and neither is your wild teenage children and your grumpy boss. Your battle is against the devil and his agents who are at work in the world today. Eph. 6:12 (NLT) says, "For we are not fighting against flesh-and-blood enemies, but against evil rulers and authorities of the unseen world."

For sure, the day the devil attacks you will come and you must be prepared at all times. To prepare for war, you've got to know the tactics the devil will use to come against you. In a battle, you need to spend time thinking about the opposition "in order that Satan may not take advantage of us; for we are not ignorant of his schemes" (2 Cor. 2:11). The devil is a liar and a deceiver. He is a cunning foe and you need to know how he operates so you'll know what to look for. You don't want to unwittingly give Satan an opening to wreak havoc in your life. Eph. 6:12 (MSG), "This is no afternoon athletic contest that we'll walk away from and forget about in a couple of hours. This is for keeps, a life-or-death fight to the finish against the devil and all his angels." The path men walk on is not easy. It's a struggle, a battle between good and evil, right and wrong. The word "wrestle" means 'to engage in as if in a violent or determined struggle.'

The devil loves it when you can't identify him. Like a cockroach he like to hide in the shadows and in the crevices of your heart. How can you fight him if you don't know he is there? He wants to remain undetected as he looks for the right opportunity to bring havoc into your life and tear you down. Many times you will be under attack and not even know it. The enemy is cunning and very crafty and if you're not careful he'll lead you to a place of complacency. He'll lull you to sleep and then rush in to destroy your life. Gen. 3:1 says, "Now the serpent was more crafty than any of the wild animals the Lord God had made. He said to the woman, "Did God say, 'You must not eat from any tree in the garden'?'" The first thing he did was place doubt in Eve's mind and this is what he is trying to do to you. He'll try to get you to question the validity of God's Word. He is a fox first, and then a lion.

He'll try to hinder you from being led by the Spirit. You'll hear something on the inside of you and the devil will get you to question if that was really God talking tor was it a figment of your imagination. One thing the devil always tries to do is take away your desire for spiritual things. The purpose of every one of his diabolical attacks is to get you separated from God. He wants you to abandon your heavenly call and start living life on your own terms. he'll try to get you to do this gradually, one little word of doubt at a time that grows slowly but surely. It's like a small crack in a dam that slowly gets bigger and bigger until the pressure is so great the dam gives way and causes flood waters to do unspeakable damage. If you'll let him, the enemy will attack you day and night in his effort to get you to lose your energy and interest for the things of God. Don't let him put your spiritual fire out.

The word "devil" means 'adversary' and he is actively and continuously hostile toward those in the body of Christ. He is a slanderer and "the accuser of the brethren" (Rev. 12:10). He is capable of shooting fiery arrows into your mind and all self-defeating thoughts come from him. He desires to make you feel guilty all the time prompting shame and remorse. If he doesn't attack you like a roaring lion, he'll attack you like a venomous snake, creeping silently along the path, endeavoring to bite your heel with his poisonous fangs. He is a liar and utters false charges that will deform and damage your reputation. He does this to weaken the power of grace and to ruin the life of godliness you are relentlessly trying to live. Job 1:7 says, "And the Lord said to Satan, 'From where do you come?' So Satan answered the Lord and said, 'From going to and fro on the earth, and from walking back and forth on it.'"

Consider Zech. 3:1, "Then he showed me Joshua the high priest standing before the Angel of the Lord, and Satan standing at his right hand to oppose him." The devil is wandering the earth looking for victims. He tried to devour Job and he'll try to devour you. Spiritual warfare is real and the enemy is not the figment of someone's imagination. This is why you need to stay sober and forever on the alert. Always be aware of his continual efforts to destroy your life. This is a very real war with real victims and real devastation. Watchfulness is the essential duty of every Christian man. The idea that the enemy may be near you at any given moment, unseen and unnoticed, is sufficient to put you on guard. Be vigilant. Keep looking all round you, watching every object lest it conceal the enemy. Watch everything with all diligence for an unwatchful man is sure to be a defeated man.

Living a defeated life should be unthinkable to a man of God. Defeat is contrary to the will of God and the promises He gives to His people. Men of God don't lose the battles they fight. They go from glory to glory, from victory to victory. A warrior knows there is no second place in a war. You're either first or you're dead. As a man of God, you are in a war with the enemy. This means you must seriously prepare for war and stay vigilant at all times. One of the best tactics of the enemy is to get men to think they are at peace when the reality is they are at war. That way he can catch them unprepared and untrained for battle. Always be prepared for war. Don't let your guard down but instead be strong and alert. You cannot afford to be passive. Too much is at stake to stand back and do nothing.

If you want peace and if you want to do damage to the kingdom of darkness, you must prepare for war and that takes initiative. In this world, battles come to us in all shapes and sizes. As long as the devil continues to roam this earth, there will be battles you must engage in. These battles come in every area of life. There will be battles against your mind, your health, your finances, and your finances. There are so many battles to fight, the best thing for you to do is be battle ready at all times. Battles require preparation, training, and lots and lots of practice. General Norman Schwarzkopf once said, "The more you sweat in peace, the less you bleed in war." To be battle ready, you must prepare for war! You can't stop the battles from coming but you can be ready when they do come. A rule of warfare is the time to be ready is not the time to get ready. You must be ready to fight your battle before the battle arrives.

The battle we are in is forever raging and all men are called to be soldiers in the army of the Lord. Demons have been released into the world and you must always be ready to go to war. We are living in a day when common sense is not so common. People are doing today what you wouldn't think of doing a generation ago. We live in a world of chaos because people are doing what is right in their own eyes. Prov. 14:12 says, "There is a way which seems right to a man, but its end is the way of death." Get ready for battle because all warriors must be prepared on all levels. First, they must be spiritually prepared because we are fighting an invisible enemy. Victories are won in the spiritual realm before they're won in the physical realm. Get on your knees and go to war for your loved ones, your fellow brethren, and for the nation you live in.

Second, warriors must be mentally prepared. When you think about it, real, intense warfare happens at its most serious level in your mind. You can't go to war with a divided mind. In Deut. 20:5-7, troops with unfinished business at home were allowed to leave. Those who were fearful and worried were also allowed to go home (vs. 8). Why? Because fear is contagious. Evil thoughts and doubts will bombard your mind every hour of every day. Discouragement will arise and frustrations will try to take over your thought life. That's why 1 Peter 1:13 (NLT) says, "So prepare your minds for action and exercise self-control." He is saying to be sober in spirit, steadfast, self-disciplined, spiritually and morally alert. Third, you must be physically prepared. When you go to war, you bring a higher level of stress into your system and your body has to be ready to handle that. Eat healthy and give your body plenty of rest.

Fourth, you've got to be prepared technically. 1 Chron. 5:18 says that the valiant men in their army were "able to bear shield and sword, to shoot with the bow, and skillful in war." They all had technical training to know how to use and handle their weapons of warfare. Likewise, your weapons are spiritual weapons and must know how to use them. Fifth, you must be financially ready. You will have a hard time focusing on fighting the enemy if you're continually worried about how to pay your bills each month. Sixth, you must be prepared familially. This means you must get your family battle ready also. When you go to war, you're not the only one in the battle. Where you go, your family goes with you. Know this, you've got to fight with everything you've got. You fight with your spirit, your mind, your words, your hands. You fight with your family, your friends, and your fellow warriors.

You fight with your diet, your money, with every resource available to you. If you have a stick, fight with it. If you have a rock, fight with it. Fight with everything you've got. You fight and then you fight some more. Your armor is not polished and nice but is tattered and worn. You don't go over the mountain in front of you, you go through it. You don't go around, under, or over your trial. You break through hat obstacle and take back what the enemy has stolen. This is why your victory is called a "breakthrough." Men everywhere should be living on the high clouds of victory, success, and spiritual fulfillment. This will happen when you "contend earnestly for the faith which was once delivered to the saints" (Jude 3). You never fight your battles from a rocking chair or a soft bed. You must be like the Greek athletes of old who exerted themselves to the point of agony in an effort to win the contest.

Never fear your enemy. That is the worst thing you can do when going into battle. Deut. 20:3 (NLT) says, "Do not be afraid as you go out to fight your enemies today! Do not lose heart or panic or tremble before them." Why? Vs. 4, "For the Lord your God is going with you! He will fight for you against your enemies, and He will give you victory!" Paul asks, "If God be for us, who can be against us?" (Rom. 8:31). Fear not! Fear not! Fear not! The Lord is with you so fear not! When the enemy comes in against you, the Spirit of the Lord "will come like a raging flood tide driven by the breath of the Lord" (Is. 59:19 NLT). The Lord is on your side. He'll fight for you and He'll give you the victory. Rom. 8:37 says, "We are more than conquerors through Him that loved us." The battle is the Lord's but the victory is yours. The devil started this fight and the blood of Jesus ended it two thousand years ago. Embrace your victory in Christ. Go to war knowing the battle has already been won (1 Cor. 15:57).

Know also there is no cease fire in the battle between good and evil. When on duty soldiers are always busy doing something. They're never idle or lazy and they never lay around doing nothing. In war you must get up and do something. You are a warrior in the army of the Lord and fighting the enemy is what you've been called to do. Sad to say, there are too many non-fighting men in the church today. Lives are being destroyed and you can't sit back and watch it happen. It's time to wake up and start fighting. Let nothing hold you back for if you don't fight the enemy will win every time. Inside of you is the power and the authority to pull down the strongholds of the enemy. You can stomp on the head of scorpions and snakes and make the devil regret the day you were born. Rise up! Storm the gates of hell and tell the enemy, "You will not prevail over my family, over my health, and over my finances! You are defeated in the name of Jesus!"

| 3 |

"THE WHOLE ARMOR"

G od doesn't want you to be ignorant of how the devil wants to take you out. 2 Cor. 2:11 says, "We would not be outwitted by Satan; for we are not ignorant of his devices." One of the most devious tactics of the devil is to convince people he doesn't exist or to trivialize his influence in the earth. As someone once said, "God is not dead, but neither is the devil." The devil is constantly on the prowl. He uses stealth as he stalks every believer. He is on the loose, roaming around seeking to trap those not watching into his evil snare. He labors to storm the castle of your heart. His temptations are called "fiery darts" (Eph. 6:16) because they often set the soul on fire. This is why the shield of faith must be raised at all times. He is called the old serpent (Rev. 12:9) for a reason. What he can't do by force, he will endeavor to do by fraud. He'll tempt the covetous man with riches and the young man with lust.

Satan will gradually tempt you to sin. He did not tell Eve bluntly to eat the apple. No, he subtly went to work asking the question, "Has God said?" He is first a fox, and then a lion. He didn't say, "God didn't say that!" He asked, "Are you sure you heard from God? Are you sure what God has said is really true?" Be careful because the devil is always trying to get you to doubt God's Word. Also, Satan is the accuser of the brethren (Rev. 12:10) and, like he did with Job, he'll accuse you of having wrong motives for loving and serving God. Another thing the devil does is twist scripture. When Jesus was in the wilderness for forty days three times the devil used scripture on Jesus to get Him to violate other scripture. The devil is a liar and a thief and he comes to steal, kill, and destroy (John 10:10). He wants to steal your joy and destroy your marriage. He wants to kill everything good in you.

Fear is one of the favorite tactics of the enemy. He prowls around like a roaring lion because he wants to scare you. He wants to frighten you so you won't take steps to fulfill your destiny. Next, he wants to deceive you. 2 Cor. 11:14 says he disguises himself as an angel of light. He'll make sin look fun and enjoyable just as he makes false teachings look authentic. Finally, he blinds people to the gospel message. 2 Cor. 4:4 says, "He has blinded the minds of unbelievers so that they will not believe the gospel of the glory of Christ." Yes, the devil does all these things but don't make the mistake of making him out to be bigger than he really is. Even though you are the target of the enemy, you don't have to tremble, fear, and worry. In fact, Rom. 16:20 says, "And the God of peace will crush Satan under your feet shortly." Notice it doesn't say God is going to crush Satan under His feet, He'll do it under your feet.

What a glorious experience it will be for you to put that evil cockroach under your foot and apply pressure until you hear the snap, crackle, pop of his demise. Never again are you to wonder what the fate of the devil is. This verse leaves no doubt as to who will be the winner in this battle. He is truly a defeated foe. Until then, the devil will not leave your situation until you make him leave. This is why you must go to war with both barrels blazing. Now is the time to show the enemy who's boss. Josh. 23:10 says, "Each of you will put to flight a thousand of the enemy, for the Lord your God fights for you, just as He has promised." With God on your side you will never be defeated. Put your nose to the grindstone and go to war knowing that victory is assured. Rom. 8:31 says, "What, then, shall we say in response to these things? If God be for us, who can be against us?"

Before you go to war, you must first learn where your strength comes from. You cannot defeat the enemy with your own might and power. You defeat him with the power that comes from on high. This is why Zech. 4:6 says, "Not by might, nor by power, but by My Spirit says the Lord." Jesus said, "You shall receive power when the Holy Spirit has come upon you" (Acts 1:8). The truth is, we were born into this world enslaved to the devil. One day Jesus looked at the Pharisees and said to them, "You are of your father the devil" (John 8:44). They thought their father was Abraham. That's how deceiving the devil is. Thankfully, Jesus came and defeated death, hell, and the grave and now we're free to become children of God. And it's in His strength that we do battle with the enemy. Paul often referred to God's mighty power in the epistles. He said in Eph. 6:10, "Be strong in the Lord and in the power of His might."

In Eph. 1:19 he tells of "the exceeding greatness of His power toward us who believe." He prayed in Eph. 3:16 that we may be "strengthened with might through His Spirit in the inner man." We do not go to war in our own strength; we do battle in the strength of the Lord. Ps. 20:7 says, "Some trust in chariots, some trust in horses; we trust in the Lord our God." The devil will say to you, "Be fearful. Look around at all the difficulties and dangers around you. Give up for you can never win." But God says, "Be strong!" Confess the words of Phil. 4:13, "I can do all things through Christ who strengthens me." Prepare for war! Be ready for battle! Be unmovable! Do not budge from the position you are taking. John Stott said, "Wobbly Christians have no foothold and are easy prey for the devil." Refuse to be pushed backward. Take your stand and offer resistance when attacked by the enemy.

In a war you must pursue a course of action with a steady aim. 1 Peter 1:13 says, "Prepare your hearts and minds for action. Stay alert and fix your hope firmly on the grace that is coming to you." Sooner or later, a Christian man will discover that life is a battleground and not a playground. Peter is saying you need to roll up your sleeves and prepare for war. 1 Cor. 16:13 says, "Be on your guard, stand firm in the faith, be courageous, be strong." Gal. 5:1 says, "Stand firm and do not let yourselves be burdened again by a yoke of slavery." Eph. 6:13 (MSG), "When it's all over but the shouting, you'll still be on your feet." Praise God, when you've finished the fight with the devil, you'll still be standing. Ps. 16:8, "I keep my eyes always on the Lord. With Him at your right hand, you will not be shaken." This is why you need to seek God like never before.

Be like the psalmist who said in Ps. 42:1, "As the deer pants for streams of water, so my soul pants for you, my God." This is not a simple thirst but rather a desperate need for something vital. Don't miss how desperate the psalmist was when he wrote these words. Deers who pant are desperate animals. This verse is the desperate cry of a man in a place of vulnerability. The good news is found in Jer. 29:13 (AMP), "Then with a deep longing you will seek Me and require of Me as a vital necessity and you will find Me when you search for Me with all your heart." To love God is to desire Him, to yearn for His righteousness, His Word, and His grace. Once you've tasted and seen that the Lord is good (Ps. 34:8), you naturally want more of Him. You'll be like Mary of Bethany who sat at the Lord's feet and listened to every word He said (Luke 10:39). To you His Word will be more precious than gold and sweeter than honey (Ps. 19;10).

To prepare for war you must prepare for victory. In Christ you are not weak, defeated, and helpless. On the contrary. Rom. 8:37 says, "We are more than conquerors through Him that loved us." Those who do fear and doubt don't have confidence in God because they don't see the victory on the other side of their trial. They look at what is seen and not what is unseen. Unbelief ties the hands of God but faith that wins believes Jesus is "far above all rule and authority, power, and dominion and every name that is named" (Eph. 1:21). Vs. 22

(NLT) says, "God has put all things under the authority of Christ and has made Him head over all things for the benefit of the church." Every man will face three enemies: the world, the flesh, and the devil himself. The good news is that Christ has overcome all these enemies, and you can too.

The way you prepare for victory is through Christ. When you raise your hands in holy surrender to Him, you will win the battle every time (1 Tim. 2:8). It is only through His strength that you will be able to stand against the enemy. Col. 2:15 says Christ "disarmed the powers and authorities, He made a public spectacle of them, triumphing over them by the cross." TPT, "Then Jesus made a public spectacle of all the powers and principalities of darkness, stripping away from them every weapon and all their spiritual authority and power to accuse us. And by the power of the cross Jesus led them around as prisoners in a procession if triumph. He was not their prisoner, they were His." The battle is the Lord's but the victory is yours. Raise your hands in praise and adoration. Focus on the Rock of your salvation, the Lamb who was slain so that you may live. Fight on your knees with your hands raised high.

Since the enemy only opposes those who are the greatest threat to him, all true men of God should forever be prepared to confront spiritual attack. You are in a war against an enemy who wants to destroy you at all costs. This is why you are called to "be strong in the Lord and in the power of His might" (Eph. 6:10). Paul is saying to be "supernaturally infused with strength through your union with Christ and to stand victorious with the force of His explosive power flowing in you and through you" (TPT). The Message Bible says, "God is strong and He wants you strong. So take everything the Master has set out for you, well-made weapons of the best material." This passage emphasizes the importance of drawing strength from God and standing firm in the face of spiritual opposition. Never back down from the enemy.

Because our adversary the devil walks about like a roaring lion you must take action. You are instructed by Paul to put on the whole armor of God (Eph. 6:11). How do you prepare for war? You put on the whole armor of God. Notice this is something you have to make an effort to do. It is your responsibility to do this. Also, according to the Greek language, this is a command and not a request. You are commanded to put on the armor of God with a sense of urgency. And once the armor is on, leave it on. Don't ever take it off. This is a battle between life and death so never let your guard down. The devil plays for keeps and so should you. Stand and watch! Never relax your vigilance for a man's sleeping time is Satan's tempting time. A soldier doesn't know when the enemy will attack but with the armor on he'll be ready at all times.

This equipment is called the armor of "God" because He both prepares and bestows it. We have no armor of our own that will be armor of proof on the day of battle. 2 Cor. 10:4 says, "The weapons we fight with are not weapons of this world. On the contrary, they have divine power to demolish strong-holds." We don't employ human weapons in this war. Our spiritual weapons are energized with divine power to effec-tively dismantle the wicked and deceiving schemes of the enemy. Calling the day the devil attacks us an "evil day" (Eph. 6:13), Paul says in vs. 14, "Stand therefore, having girded your waist with truth." We must first put on the belt of truth which means to wholeheartedly accept God's Word and His faithfulness in the fulfillment of His promise as exhibited in Christ.

Every piece of armor the Roman soldiers wore was fastened to his belt. The foundation of all we do is to be based on truth. A dishonest man cannot hope to withstand the father of lies. Paul next says to "put on the breastplate of righteousness" (vs. 14). The breastplate protects the heart and all the vital parts of the body. Righteousness can be defined as that gracious gift of God to man whereby all who believe on the Lord Jesus Christ are brought into a right relationship with God. Righteousness is that which conforms itself to the revealed will of God. To win a war a soldier must be well armed for battle but if inwardly he has not a good heart his armor will be of little use to him. Godly men are people of integrity. They're morally upright and are without sin and guilt. No spiritual protection is greater than a righteous relationship with God.

The next piece of armor we are to put on is found in Eph. 6:15 (NLT), "For shoes, put on the peace that comes from the Good News so that you will be fully prepared." The gospel of peace enables you to walk with a steady pace in the way of the Lord without being hindered or overcome by the difficulties and dangers that may be on the path we are traveling. To be ready for combat you must not be easily provoked nor prone to be quarrelsome. The Bible says we are peacemakers. You must show gentleness and long-suffering to all men. Is. 52:7 says,

"How beautiful upon the mountains are the feet of him who bring good news, who proclaims peace, who brings good tidings of good things." Peace is the result of the spiritual prosperity that comes with a harmonious walk with God and is also the evidence of faith. If you are walking by faith, you will have peace (Heb. 4:3).

Next, Eph. 6:16 says, "Above all, taking the shield of faith, with which you will be able to quench all the fiery darts of the wicked one." A Roman shield was huge and covered the whole body which the soldier could hide behind when the enemy shot their arrows at him. What are some of the arrows the devil shoots at us? Accusation. Guilt. Doubt. Disobedience. Rebellion. These are but a few of the woes that can be quenched with the shield of faith. This is why faith is central in the life of every man. It doesn't take much faith to receive from God. It just takes active faith. 1 John 5:4 says, "For everyone born of God overcomes the world. This is the victory that has overcome the world, even our faith."

Eph. 6:17 (NLT) says, "Put on salvation as your helmet." To wear the helmet of salvation means to know that your salvation is absolutely secure and complete. The head is the seat of your mind. The desire of the enemy is to attack your mind and tempt you to despair but a good hope keeps you trusting in God and rejoicing in Him. Knowing you are saved will protect you from thoughts of guilt and condemnation. Is. 26:3 (AMP), "You will guard him and keep him in perfect peace whose mind is stayed on You." Hope is the confident and favorable expectation of future good. A good hope will comfort the soul and keep your mind from being troubled and tormented by the storms that come your way. Paul wrote in 1 Thess. 5:8 to put on "as a helmet the hope of salvation." A well founded and well built hope will both purify the soul and keep it from being defiled by the enemy.

Many people struggle because in their minds they think their storms are bigger than God. It is for this reason that Paul tells us to "be transformed by the renewing of your mind" (Rom. 12:2). This comes about when we use the only offensive weapon in the armor of God called "the sword of the Spirit, which is the Word of God" (Eph. 6:17). God's Word is an indispensable weapon. The Amplified Bible says in Heb. 4:12 that the Word is "alive and full of power - making it active, operative, energizing and effective." To win your battle you must continually use the sword of the Spirit and say what God says. In the wilderness, Jesus resisted the temptations of Satan by saying, "It is written..." (Matt. 4:4,7,10). When you confess the Word over your storm, the enemy will flee and the rough waters and blowing wind will become peaceful and still. That is what victory is all about.

| 4 |

"FERVENT IN SPIRIT"

Real men are spoiling for a fight because they know the enemy prevails when good men do nothing. They wake up each morning knowing they can't let the destruction of the enemy continue. They know something has to be done in the times we now live. All over the world God is raising up a mighty army of men to combat the devil and all those under his dominion. Real men are not begrudgingly forced into battle. No, they go to war willingly. Ps. 110:3 says, "Your people shall be volunteers in the day of Your power." They fight with confidence knowing the gates of hell will not prevail against them (Matt. 16:18). They are empowered with God's mighty strength. They are majestic in holiness, arrayed in the King's armor. In the splendor of holiness and spiritual purity they are dressed for battle and eager to serve God and participate in the work He is doing. It is for His glory and honor that they fight.

Daily they present themselves as a free-will offering to the Lord. They are like a mist, arising from the dawn of a new spiritual awakening, providing protection for the world they live in. This is the day of God's power and it's time for all the men of God to arise. You are in the army of the Lord and your marching orders are to "rule in the midst of your enemies" (Ps. 110:2). The problem today is too many men are asleep to the urgency of the hour. People's lives are being destroyed by the enemy and the men of God are taking a nap. Most men are sleeping giants. They're like a bear in hibernation as they sit back and wait for somebody else to fix the problem. What does God say about this? Joel 3:9 says, "Prepare for war! Wake up the mighty men, let all the men of war draw near, let them come up." It's time to prepare for war! It's time for the mighty men of God to wake up!

Rom. 13:11 (NLT) says, "This is all the more urgent, for you know how late it is; time is running out. Wake up, for our salvation is nearer now than when we first believed." Now is time for men to wake up from the "sleep of spiritual complacency" (AMP). Too many men are more worried about their next golf game than their neighbor who is perishing and on their way to hell. God is raising up a different breed of men, men who will prepare for war and do something about the chaos the world is now in. He's raising up men who know when they move, God moves. The world today needs men like the saints of old who were so burdened for the cause of God that they did powerful works that would bewilder those living in this current age. These saints were rock solid in their refusal to go forward without a word from God. They wept and mourned for days at a time over the backslidden condition of God's people.

They were different from everyone else. They refused to eat, drink, or wash their bodies. They tore out clumps of hair from their scalp and beard. It mattered to them when God was not glorified. How many men today would follow the example of the prophet Jeremiah who laid on his side in the streets of Jerusalem for 365 days continually warning of God's coming judgment? The Bible says all these things they did were recorded as examples for us to follow (1 Cor. 10:11). There was something about their character that caused God to lay His hand on them. If ever there was a time when the world needed godly men to rise up and go to war it is now. Our present generation is many times worse than it was in the days of Sodom and Gomorrah. God is looking for men who will strive to know His heart and do mighty exploits in His name, men who will go to war and carry His burden and speak for His cause.

Strive to be like Ezra who testified, "I was strengthened as the hand of the Lord my God was upon me" (Ezra 7:28). God stretched out His hand and turned Ezra into a different man. What prompted God to do this? Ezra 7:10 says, "Ezra had prepared his heart to seek the law of the Lord, and to do it." He made a conscious decision to act on everything he read. God saw in Ezra a man totally absorbed in His Word. Ezra hungered for the scriptures and rejoiced in them. He allowed them to prepare his heart for any work God chose for him. This is why God laid His hand on Ezra and anointed him. No man can expect God's touch on his life if he isn't passionate about the scriptures like Ezra was. If you want to be used by God, then you must first have a deep love and affection for the Word of

God. Ps. 119:140 says, "Your word is very pure; Therefore Your servant loves it."

Love the Word and you'll be ready for battle. God is looking for a few good men, men like Jonathan who said, "For nothing restrains the Lord from saving by many or by few" (1 Sam. 14:6). You can't have the mentality of a civilian who sits on the sidelines and does nothing. You're not here to wile away the hours just to see how much fun you can have or how many toys you can buy. Stop seeking comfort all the time but look for battles to be fought. You're a warrior and fighting is what you do. You're a soldier in the army of the Lord and you'll go anywhere, at any time, at any cost. We've all been called to be warriors in the army of the Lord. When the call comes the only acceptable response is "Here I am! Send me" (Is. 6:8). When you put your hand to the plow, never look back to the fleeting pleasures this life has to offer. Always "press toward the goal for the upward call of God in Christ Jesus" (Phil. 3:14).

In this evil world, something has to be done. Ask God to tell you what His marching orders are for your life. Tell Him you'll fight in the rain, the snow, and in 110 degree heat. Tell Him you'll crawl in the mud, run in a storm, eat out of a can, sleep under the stars, carry heavy equipment, and go long hours without rest or sleep. A soldier is conditioned for obedience and with much vigilance puts priority on his calling and the task at hand. Be willing to go where God tells you to go and stay where He tells you to stay. In the army of the Lord, you cannot be idle. When on duty, soldiers are always busy doing something. They're never inactive or lazy and they never lay around and do nothing. You must wake up and prepare for war. 1 Cor. 3:9 says "we are God's fellow workers." We are laborers in the kingdom of God and work is what we've been called to do.

The world is going to hell in a hand basket and some men justify it when they sit back and do nothing. It is high time for these men to wake up from their slumber and spiritual inactivity. Something has to be done and God is calling all men to rise up and make this world a better place. Rom. 12:11 (NLT) says, "Never be lazy in your work but serve the Lord enthusiastically." The Philips Bible says, "Let us not allow slackness to spoil our work, and let us keep the fires of our spirit burning as we do our work for the Lord." This is a rebuke to passivity, laziness, lethargy, apathy, and boredom. The Amplified Bible says, "Never lag in zeal, and in earnest endeavor be aglow and burning with the Spirit serving the Lord." You are to serve the Lord with genuine commitment. Have a zeal and eagerness that cannot be contained. Be diligent with a readiness to expend energy and effort.

Always be fervent in spirit. The Greek word for "fervent" is "zeo" and it means 'boil; to be hot; burn; and glow.' This means you must be earnest, zealous, on fire, and enthusiastic in serving the Lord. Never let your zeal burn out and wither away but forever maintain that spiritual glow that comes when you faithfully do what you've been called to do. This Greek word paints a picture of a person so enthusiastic about their work for the Lord they can hardly contain their excitement. They can't wait to wake up each and every morning. Their desire to do God's work with excellence and enthusiasm is constantly boiling inside, creating a Holy Spirit controlled and empowered diligence regarding their divine assignment. Our purpose for living is to complete our tour of duty. We're in the trenches with devils and diseases. We're here to rub elbows with those who are hurting and need a friend to lean on.

We are not here just to have a good time. We're in the trenches with devils and diseases. We're here to rub elbows with those who are hurting and need a friend to lean on. We are here to make a positive difference in the world and our love for God is shown in our service to other people. Ask God to give you a vision bigger than yourself. Ask Him to make you a difference-maker. Don't be a talker, be a walker. Be a man who gets results. If you don't do this, God will find somebody who will. You don't want that to happen. Get out of your comfort zone. Wake up and prepare for war! Let God get a hold of you! Let Him ignite the fire inside of you! You were born to be great. You were born to love and called to serve. This is greatness in the eyes of God. To be great you must forever be striving with diligence and holy fervor to make this world a better place. Inside of you is an intensity that makes you want to serve the Lord with a spirit that is fueled and aflame.

God is calling you to do something great. With fervor and enthusiasm you must find ways to pour yourself into the things of God. "Set your mind on things above, not on things on the earth" (Col. 3:2). TPT, "Yes, feast on all the treasures of the heavenly realm and fill your thoughts with heavenly realities, and not with the distractions of the natural realm." This is something that must be done on purpose. Set your will to daily, moment by moment, think about and direct your minds toward the things of heaven and eternity. All your thoughts must abide in heaven and not on the earth. Have nothing to do with mundane things but give your heart and soul to heavenly things, thinking always about that which is above. Let the things of God and His assignment for your life fill your thoughts. Constantly meditate on the things God would have you do to help make the lives of other people better.

Archibald A. T. Robertson said, "The Christian has to keep his feel upon the earth but his head in the heavens. He must be heavenly minded here on earth and to make the earth like heaven." Launch each new day with the mindset that you will diligently work toward the fulfillment of your destiny. Do that and life for you will be one great adventure. German theologian Johann Bengel said in the 18th century, "They who truly seek the things that are above cannot but relish or set their affection on the things that are above." We are in the world but not of the world. 1 Peter 2:11 says we are aliens and strangers here. This is why we must filter everything we see and experience through the lens of eternity. Charles Spurgeon said, "True hearts in this wicked world are all too apt to swerve, but still they show their inward and persistent tendency to point toward heaven and God."

Prepare for war! Be white hot! Boil with heat! Have a burning zeal to do the will of God. With fervor and enthusiasm you must find ways to pour yourself into the things of God. Daily you are to live for God's honor and glory. Rom. 14:8 (TPT) says, "While we live, we must live for the Master, and in death we must bring honor to Him. So dead or alive we belong to our Master." Those who have lost their fervency and passion for doing God's work have become empty, slack, shallow, sluggish, and useless. No longer do they have a purpose for living. People in the Old Testament were warned about being lazy, complacent, carefree, and slothful. Amos 6:1 says, "Woe to you who are at ease in Zion." You were put on this earth to serve God, not to please yourself. The greatest honor you can give to Him is the service the scriptures require you to render to the Redeemer.

Why are we here? Charles Spurgeon said, "We remain on earth as sowers to scatter good seed; as ploughmen to break up the fallow ground; as heralds publishing salvation. We are here as the salt of the earth, to be a blessing to the world. We are here to glorify Christ in our daily life. Let us live earnest, useful, holy lives to the praise of the glory of His grace." There is a work to be done! The Father works, the Son works, and you are to work also. Jesus said in John 5:17, "My Father has been working until now, and I have been working." Paul said in 1 Cor. 15:58, "Be steadfast, immovable, always abounding in the work of the Lord, knowing that your labor is not in vain in the Lord." The Amplified Bible says, "Always being superior, excelling, doing more than enough in the service to the Lord." Paul is saying to always give yourself fully to the work of the Lord.

Don't drag your feet spiritually but be full of zeal and enthusiasm. The heat of your fervency will drive you forward and cause you to wake up each morning ready and willing to be used by God. Jesus said in Matt. 5:16, "Let your light so shine before men, that they may see your good works and glorify your Father in heaven." This is a great motivator to be fervent in spirit. The brighter and hotter your light shines, the more glory the Father receives. Prepare for war knowing that nothing can stop the man who is fired up with zeal and enthusiasm. Be a man who is full of a fiery anointing that empowers him in everything he does. Be a man driven by compassion with an irresistible motivation that gives your life direction and meaning. Paul said in 2 Cor. 5:14, "The love of Christ compels me." MSG, "Christ's love has moved me to such extremes." Fervor and enthusiasm are the fundamental keys to success in a man's service to the Lord.

Fervency produces results (James 5:10) and gives boldness and power (Acts 18:25-28). It brings rejoicing to God's people (2 Cor. 7:6-8) and makes up for other shortcomings (1 Peter 4:8; Jude 22). Most of all, fervency brings about a real and genuine love (1 Peter 1:22), a love that stays on fire and never burns out or grows cold (Matt. 24:12). A fervent spirit burns for God in such a way that you are consumed by Him. He is the reason you wake up in the morning. He is your one and only, your all in all. In Him you live and move and have your being (Acts 17:28). Work for God with feeling and live for Him with all your might. Intensity matters. Zeal matters (Jer. 29:13,14). Don't settle for anything less. Work for God passionately and be eager to accomplish what He has called you to do. Serving God is not for the weak and timid. It takes strength to be diligent so let the weak say "I am strong" (Joel 3:10).

Wake up and prepare for war! The end of the age is upon us so stop sitting on the sidelines of manhood. Go out and do something good with your life. Don't lay your weapons down! This is not a time of peace; it's a time of war. The enemy we fight takes no prisoners. He knows all he has to do to win this war is get the men of God to do nothing. This is why he is relentless in his pursuit to keep the men of God silent and inoperative in the world today. Don't let this happen to you. Rise up and let your voice be heard. Joel 3:16 says, "And the Lord shall roar from Zion, and utter His voice from Jerusalem; and the heavens and the earth shall shake." God roars and you should too! Jesus is the Lion of the tribe of Judah (Rev. 5:5) and Joel portrays Him as a hungry lion who roars with his thunderous voice as he rushes to leap on its helpless prey.

Joel 2:11 says, "The Lord utters His voice before His army; Surely His camp is very great, for strong is he who carries out His Word. The day of the Lord is indeed great and very awesome." Jer. 25:30 says, "The Lord will roar from on high, and utter His voice from His holy habitation." In other words, the time of being silent is over! Don't let the enemy lull you to sleep! Wake up and prepare for war! Ignite the fire! Be a voice that cries in the wilderness and in the city. Don't let the devil silence you. Don't let him put your fire out. Jesus said, "You are the light of the world. A city that is set on a hill cannot be hidden" (Matt. 5:14). Live a life that lights up the world with God's glory. In the world today there are giants that must be taken down. Wake up and run toward those giants. Bring the presence of God into this evil generation. If you don't, God will raise up someone who will.

| 5 |

"SEIZE THE MOMENT"

The moment you put your faith and trust in Jesus Christ a great miracle occurred. He took you out of darkness and placed you into His marvelous light. But that is not all that happened. Not only did He bring you into His family, He also enlisted you into His army. Every born again man is a soldier in the Lord's army. Face the fact that you are in the Lord's army. That's not the question. The question is, "Are you a good soldier in the Lord's army? Can you be counted on to do your duty?" The Greek word for "good" is "kalos" and it refers to what is genuinely and inherently good, organically healthy, fit, useful, and serviceable. It means to be free from defects like a bar of gold that is pure and genuine. It's the total state of soundness, wholeness and order, and to be morally sound.

To be a good soldier you must dedicate yourself to a life of unwavering faith, obedience, and service. A good soldier follows orders and serves a higher purpose. A good soldier is prepared to endure hardness and suffering for the sake of their cause. They're called to persevere in their faith even when facing challenges and persecution. Good soldiers need discipline and self-control to perform their duties effectively. Roman soldiers were a model of discipline and because of that they were unbeatable. A good soldier must be courageous for they are called to stand firm in their beliefs and their trust in God's power. They fight to win and are therefore steadfast at all times. The good soldier's greatest desire is to please God, to receive the unfading crown of glory, to hear his Master say, "Well done, good and faithful servant" (Matt. 25:21).

Many men live their life for enjoyment, not for service. They go to church only to hear sermons that make them feel good. They despise messages that require something of them. The Bible paints a different picture of what a Christian man should look like. It envisions a man not sitting at a banquet table but with a sword strapped to his side, ready for battle. A real man is not lazy. He doesn't lay down on the softest beds sleeping through life in blissful serenity. No, he is a soldier with hard, demanding work to do. The mark of a true, dedicated soldier is to wear bloodstained garments. He carries hacked swords, dented armor, and bruised shields. He is and forever will be a man of action. His life is far from luxurious. In the stillness of the night, when he is the most exhausted, the trumpet may sound calling him to battle when he would prefer to stay home and rest.

A soldier is a servant, not living for his own pleasure. A good soldier must be self-sacrificing and ready at all times to lay down his life for the King he serves. A good soldier must be prepared to suffer, enduring hardship after hardship, not seeking worldly pleasures but finding joy and satisfaction in fighting for Christ's sake. 2 Tim. 2:3 says, "You therefore must endure hardness as a good soldier of Jesus Christ." MSG, "When the going gets rough, take it on the chin like the rest of us, the way Jesus did." We are in a battle against an enemy who comes to steal, kill, and destroy (John 10:10). In this battle we don't run and hide from the enemy, we prepare for war and attack the enemy. 2 Tim. 1:7 says, "For God has not given us a spirit of fear, but of power and of love and of a sound mind." Don't fear the enemy but "be strong in the grace that is in Jesus Christ" (2 Tim. 2:1).

Paul does not urge Timothy to be just an ordinary soldier, but to be a "good soldier of Jesus Christ." Not all soldiers are good soldiers. In fact, there are three kinds of soldiers in the Lord's army. The young soldier has the will to fight. He is anxious to go into battle. However, experience in fighting is lacking. The young soldier has zeal without knowledge. The old soldier has experience in fighting. However, the will to fight is missing. He has knowledge without zeal. The good soldier has both the will to fight and experience in fighting. He has the right combination of zeal and knowledge. A good soldier is a champion for the cause of Christ. The word "good" means 'valuable, virtuous, worthy.' A good soldier is the bravest of the brave, courageous at all times. He is zealous, performing his duties with heart and earnestness, striving always to bring glory to God.

A good soldier is loyal to the King and obedient to his Captain's commands. He is self-sacrificing and serves at all times. His greatest passion is to conquer at all costs. A good soldier battles for peace. He pulls down strongholds so that the humble and the meek may be established in their walk with God and the ministry He calls them to. Philosopher Lucius Seneca said in the first century AD, "To live is to be a soldier." A soldier is a soldier and nothing else. A good soldier enlists for warfare and active duty. Their minds are girded for action (1 Peter 1:13). They're always watching and praying (Matt. 26:41), they're sober in spirit (2 Tim. 4:5), and they are always on alert (1 Thess. 5:6). A good soldier must have courage because the more faithful they are, the more their enemies will multiply. Their enemies are the enemies of God and they must be bold and fight at all times.

A soldier in the Lord's army is forever loyal to his King. On the day he enlisted he put his finger in the Lord's nail-scarred hand and said like Thomas, "My Lord and my God." He acknowledges Jesus as his King and his heart is full of loving devotion to Him. Nothing makes his heart leap like the mention of His wonderful and glorious name. Is. 9:6 says, "And His name will be called Wonderful, Counselor, Mighty God, Everlasting Father, Prince of Peace." This is the God he serves, the God he will be forever loyal to. Each and every day his role an a soldier of the Lord is to build up and advance the kingdom of God, to maintain His authority, and to exalt the glory of His name. Good soldiers take an oath to never desert their standard, to submit their will to the commands of their leader. They are ready and willing to sacrifice their life for the God they're fighting for.

The training of a soldier is designed to make him obey the word of command with no questions asked. He never asks "Why?" He just does what he is commanded to do. In a bloody war centuries ago a general told his men they must not retreat but hold their position at all costs. The men said, "That means we must all die." The general answered, "Precisely!" A good soldier obeys orders no matter what the cost may be. He is conditioned to loyalty. His supreme virtue is that he is faithful unto death. They never dream of turning their backs and running away when the enemy is coming. You cannot be a true warrior without possessing a loyal devotion to God which springs from love. A good general makes good soldiers. He infuses his own spirit into them and leads them to victory. We have a good general. Put yourself in His hands and He'll make you the good soldier you ought to be.

In Shakespeare's play 'Henry IV,' Prince Hal is about to embark on a military campaign and he is determined to prove himself as a worthy leader and a brave soldier. He knows that in a war there is no turning back and he is quoted as saying, "Cursed be the sun if it sets today and sees me retreat" (Act 2, Scene 4). This quote expresses his fierce determination and refusal to allow any setback or retreat to blemish his reputation and his ambition. He curses the sun if it sets and witnesses his failure. A good soldier is determined to win or die on the battlefield. He sees difficulties only as challenges to overcome. No matter how hard the task, he presses forward anyway. They press on because inside of them is a passion for victory, an unending hunger to establish the throne of God in the hearts of men near and far.

These are warriors who know that true manhood is a fight. Let no man say he has no taste for war. Sad to say, thousands of men go to church every week but they never enter spiritual battle. They want their pastor and their wives to do the fighting for them. These men are passive cowards. All they want to do is live a life of religious ease, laziness, idleness, and security. To be a real man is to become a man of war. The true man of God is called to be a soldier and must behave as such from the day of his conversion to the day of his death. He must never imagine for a moment that he can sleep and doze his way to heaven. No, he must fight! Let us not think we can remain neutral and do nothing. Each one of us bears the sign of the cross which binds us to be Christ's soldiers till the day we go home to heaven. Let us remember the Name under which we serve. To Him we are faithful unto death.

A good soldier is always brave in battle. Though a thousand arrows are flying toward him, he considers it an honor to be fighting for his King. Good soldiers don't know how to yield and give up when the going gets tough. They hold tightly onto their sword with the goal of overcoming all that stands in their way. In the book of Revelation, there are no promises in the Lord's letters to the seven churches except to those who overcome. This tells us that in a war, heroic effort and patient endurance is necessary. Spiritual warfare is no light matter. A wise general once said, "In time of war it is the worst mistake to underrate your enemy and try to make a little war." Jesus said in Matt. 10:34, "Do not think that I have come to bring peace to the earth. I have not come to bring peace, but a sword." A sword brings division and that is why we're here.

He said in vs. 35, "For I have come to set a man against his father, a daughter against her mother, and a daughter-in-law against her mother-in-law." Jesus is warning His followers that His teachings will cause division and conflict, not only between family members but between those who follow Him and those who don't. This passage is not a call to violence or disrespect toward family matters, but rather a warning about the potential for conflict and division that can arise because of your beliefs. Yes, Jesus is the great Peacemaker but before peace He brings war. Truth abides and it cannot and will not lower its standard which means falsehood must be trodden under foot. Charles Spurgeon said, "If you follow Christ, you shall have all the dogs of the world yelping at your heels." This is why Jesus said in Luke 22:36, "Whoever has no sword is to sell his coat and buy one."

The lesson here is that true manhood is a struggle, a fight, a war. When there is grace, there will be conflict. The necessity of warfare is upon all of us and we must prepare for war and fight. No matter what the consequences may be, you must always do what is right. You will need the courage of a lion to live a life that will turn your closest friend into your fiercest enemy. You can win this war because a good soldier gets his strength from on high. They are "strong in the Lord and in the power of His might" (Eph. 6:10). This is how victory is achieved. Fellowship with Christ is the fountain of a man's strength. Go to Him and say, "Lord, I will do the work You sent me to do if You will give me a measure of Your conquering power." With God's strength you will shine like stars forever and ever. Never will you fall away from your high calling.

Never will you pull back but will only go forward in the fervor of your zeal.

To be a good soldier you must freely engage in His service with great enthusiasm. Every believing man is a soldier. Saved souls will always be found to have fought a good fight. Be relentless with renewed energy and put forth a greater exertion for the cause of Christ. Let the vision of the victory that awaits you be the motivation to forever press forward. Never let the high standard of your work, virtue, and spiritual attainment dwindle because of the presence of war. Instead, be the best soldier you can be, doing as much for Christ as you can possibly do. Let your life reflect the power that is at work inside of you. Now is the time for war. It's time to be vigilant, to be fervent with unwavering faith and relentless dedication. Seize the moment and glorify God by spreading His truth far and wide. The Lord is on your side so go forward knowing "God is our refuge and strength, a very present help in trouble" (Ps. 46:1).

In a moment of courage that stands out in biblical history, David approached King Saul with a bold declaration of his intent to combat the threatening giant Goliath. He knew he would not be forsaken by his God so he said to Saul. "Let no man's heart fail because of him. Your servant will go and fight with this Philistine" (1 Sam. 17:32). Here was a young shepherd boy who applied his faith as a source of strength where others trembled in fear. The Lord was his shepherd and he had no fear of defeat. David showed all of us that "with God nothing shall be impossible" (Luke 1:37). With God's help you can go to war and stand your ground with faith and be triumphant. This young giant of a man said to Goliath, "And all this assembly shall know that the Lord saves not with sword or spear, for the battle is the Lord's, and He will give you into our hands" (vs. 47).

David drew strength for his faith from the promise found in Deut. 20:1 that says God is the source of all power and is the one who determines the outcomes of the battles we fight. On that great day in the Valley of Elah God used the physically weakest of the family of Jesse to display His power and might before the world bringing Him much glory. The battles we fight belong to the Lord and all we do is participate in His victory. God will turn every circumstance around for good and what looks hopeless will become a victory in Christ. You are a soldier in the Lord's army and the battles you face are His battles. David did not fear the giant before him and his victory came from the Lord's power and intervention. It was David who wrote in Ps. 56:3,4, "Whenever I am afraid, I will trust in You. In God I have put my trust; I will not fear. What can man do to me?"

A Christian man must forever concentrate on his manhood and use whatever task he is engaged in to demonstrate his devotion to his Commander-In-Chief. A good soldier is one who does not do minimum duty for his Lord but rather is one who serves Him with everything he is and everything he has. That is his calling. He's like Paul who said in Acts 20:24 (TPT), "I don't esteem my life as indispensable. It's more important for me to fulfill my destiny and to finish the ministry the Lord Jesus has assigned to me." Every day he puts his life on the line in the service to his Master. He is ready and willing to deny himself, take up his cross, and follow Jesus wherever it may take him. War is hard and tough. There is suffering in warfare. It's not like a Sunday stroll on a beach. Soldiers don't fight at the playground; they fight on the battleground.

Have confidence in God for He leads the charge in every battle you face. With God on your side victory is assured every time. If God be for us, who can be against us? In a time of war British Army officer Sir Colin Campbell received a message that Her Majesty's guards were under heavy attack and was asked if they should bull back to safer quarters. Without hesitation he answered, "It were better, sir, that every one of Her Majesty's guards should be dead on this battlefield than turn their backs on the enemy." And so it is with those in the Lord's army. It would be far better to die on the battlefield than live a coward's life. May you never feel the shame of running away when Goliath crosses your path. The victory is before you so press forward and grab onto it. Seek out your own sphere of action and give yourself wholly to it. Let nothing stop you from fulfilling your destiny.

| 6 |

"THE FRONT LINES"

S piritual warfare is as real and true as any war the world has ever seen. Like it or not, it is a war which every man who would be saved must fight. The life of a true Christian man of God comes with hatred from the world. Jesus said in John 15:18, "If this world hates you, you know that it has hated Me before it hated you." He then said in vs. 20, "A servant is not greater than his master. If they persecuted Me, they will also persecute you." Don't expect the world to stand up and clap because you've devoted your life to Jesus Christ. On the contrary, they'll hate you for it. The world won't like it when your light reveals their sin and corruption. Except for John, all the disciples and Paul were killed for their faith. Legend has it that John was boiled in oil for what he believed in. That was probably a worse punishment than death. Going AWOL is not an option for a good soldier is willing to suffer hardship like Jesus did.

A good soldier endures hardness. They also remained focused at all times. 2 Tim. 2:4 says, "No soldier in active service entangles himself in the affairs of everyday life." Why? "So that he may please the one who enlisted him as a soldier." A good soldier can't be consumed and distracted by everyday life. A good soldier is on a mission and he's in the Lord's army for a purpose. He's in a tour of duty and he has a job to do. Good soldiers don't go somewhere to live, they go to fight. They complete the mission and then go home. This world is not our home. We're citizens of heaven on a mission with the Lord (Phil. 3:20). Jesus said in Matt. 28:19 (NLT), "Therefore, go and make disciples of all the nations." Vs. 20 (NLT), "Teach these new disciples to obey all the commands I have given you." Your mission is to shine for Christ and share the gospel message with others.

Paul told Timothy that all soldiers are to be in active service. This means they are to perform military service and be prepared to go to war at a moment's notice. Eccl. 8:8 says, "There is no discharge in the time of war." Active service calls for rigorous self-discipline, unquestioning obedience, and a willingness to die for the cause you fight for. The Greek word "strateuomai" means 'to make a military expedition, to do military duty, be on active service, to be engaged in warfare.' A good soldier is on duty around the clock. For him, going to battle against the enemy is a lifestyle and not an occasional endeavor. Even when on leave he is subject to recall. All that he is belongs to the military in which he serves. When ordered to go to war he is expected to put his life on the line without question or hesitation.

Total commitment is necessary in order to be a good soldier. Military service involves self-sacrifice, discipline, vigilance, obedience, enthusiasm, and much loyalty. His service to the King must be a concentrated service. No longer can he be entangled with the daily business of ordinary life for he must concentrate on his role as a soldier. He is conditioned to obedience no matter what risks he is ordered to take. The early training of a soldier is designed to make him obey the word of command without question. His allegiance is to the God he serves and his primary duty is to obey the voice of God and to accept his assignment even if it is something he does not fully understand. He trusts that God knows everything and sees the end from the beginning (Is. 46:10). It is not his responsibility to know the reason why a particular order is given.

Many men think they can be a Christian and not have to fight as a soldier. They are deceiving themselves for all men are on the front lines of battle whether they realize it or not. All men are called to rise up and do something great for God. Make no mistake about it, you were not created to just exist and try to get in touch with your feelings. Most men today are bored and there is nothing worse than a bored man. This is why the Bible says it's time to wake him up! It's time to prepare for war and wake up something inside of you. Wake up what? Wake up the mighty man! If you don't, you'll live life without purpose. You'll drift from one fleshly pleasure to the next. Too many men are sitting down with a beer in one hand and a TV remote in the other. They're silent about what they believe in. They think silence is golden so they say nothing. They need to wake up and speak up.

It is spineless to not proclaim the gospel message, especially when people are waiting for someone to stand up and give them the wisdom they need. God has called us to speak up with wisdom and love. Jesus said in Mark 16:15, "Go into all the world and preach the gospel to every creature." When in combat you're supposed to stay focused on the task at hand. Heb. 12:1 (NLT), "Let us strip off every weight that slows us down, especially the sin that so easily trips us up." It then says, "And let us run with endurance the race God has set before us." Vs. 2 (NLT), "We do this by keeping our eyes on Jesus, the champion who initiates and perfects our faith." In a war, you take your eyes off of everything else and fix your eyes on Jesus. You focus on Him at all times. You don't live for the approval of others; you live for the approval of Jesus and Him only.

You're here to please the one who enlisted you as a soldier, that person being the Lord Jesus Christ. You're here to please Him in everything you do. That's what the life of a good soldier is all about. How do you please the one King of kings and Lord of lords? You please Him by being faithful to Him. 1 Cor. 4:2 says, "Moreover it is required of stewards that one be found faithful." The Amplified Bible says, "A man should be found faithful proving himself worthy of trust." Be faithful. Be reliable. Be trustworthy. Don't go AWOL but man your post. The word "trustworthy" means 'to be steadfast in one's affection or allegiance, being loyal to a cause or a person, being constant, persistent, and faithful.' Notice it doesn't say be found fruitful, but to be found faithful. God will take care of the fruit if we are faithful for He alone causes the growth (1 Cor. 3:6).

Paul called Timothy his "beloved and faithful child in the Lord" (1 Cor. 4:17). To be faithful means to be reliable, steadfast, and unwavering. Let this describe the type of person you are. God is looking for men of character He can trust, men who walk consistently with Him and are in humble service to Him. God calls all men to be faithful and let the chips fall where they may. Be faithful at all times. Go where God tells you to go and stay where God tells you to stay. Do what you're called to do. Don't be like King Saul who lost his kingdom because he wasn't faithful to the Lord. He acted on what the people under him wanted more than on what God wanted. Be a good steward of what God has given you. 1 Tim. 6:20 says, "Timothy, guard what God has entrusted to you." When the Lord returns the only absolute requirement by which He will judge His servants is faithfulness (Matt. 24:45,46). Were they true to the Lord's commands?

Jesus said in Rev. 2:10, "Do not fear any of those things which you are about to suffer. Be faithful until death and I will give you the crown of life." Yes, you will suffer persecution in this life but you must remain faithful. You can do that if you know that, as in the case of Job, God puts limits to constrain what Satan can do to you. This is the only place in the Bible where we are commanded to be faithful. This verse encourages endurance and unwavering commitment to God even in the face of hardship. This is a call to action, urging all men to live out their faith wholeheartedly and not to compromise their principles. Be faithful and you'll find peace regardless of your circumstances. All good soldiers let nothing stop them from fulfilling their mission. They know when you are prepared to die for the cause of Christ, you will be most prepared to live for Him.

The mighty men of God are faithful and always prepared for war because they know ease and comfort are nowhere promised as a reward for their faith. John MacArthur said, "The crown of genuine saving faith is eternal life, and perseverance proves the genuineness of their faith as they endure suffering." The fight you're in requires diligent training, energy, and strong exertion. The pace will be fast and the going hard. There will be sweat and pain and for some death. Do not fear but be faithful at all times, faithful until death. Trust in God and let Him be your strength and courage. Fight boldly knowing it is the Lord you are fighting for. And when the war is over you'll stand before the King of kings and Lord of lords. In His hand is the victor's crown which every conqueror will have placed on his head.

A good soldier stays focused and doesn't get entangled with the things of this world. He lives for the approval of the Commander-In-Chief and remains faithful to Him always and forever. If you'll remain faithful, God will give you the grace to serve Him and complete your mission. 2 Tim. 2:1 says, "You, therefore, my son, be strong in the grace that is in Christ Jesus." TPT says, "Timothy, my dear son, life your life empowered by God's free-flowing grace, which is your true strength, found in the anointing of Jesus and your union with Him." Charles Spurgeon said, "This is an exhortation to every one of us, not only to have grace, but to be strong in it. Never be content with just being saved and barely alive spiritually." The greatest need of every soldier is to be empowered for battle, to be continually strengthened with inner strength by means of the grace which is in Christ Jesus.

Paul is saying you must be clothed with inner strength. Let God make you strong with the special grace and favor that can only be found in the Lord Jesus Christ. The Greek word for "be strong" is "endunamoo" and it means 'to put power in and thus to make strong or vigorous, to be strengthened, enabled, and empowered.' Judges 6:34 says, "So the Spirit of the Lord came upon Gideon." The words "came upon" means 'to wrap around, to put on a garment, to figuratively clothe oneself with the Holy Spirit.' No man can be a good soldier and serve successfully in the power of his own flesh. This is why we're told to "be strong in the Lord and in the power of His might" (Eph. 6:10). Apart from God's power and enablement, the man of God, no matter how sincere and diligent he is, can accomplish nothing of eternal value that brings glory to God.

To be useful in God's kingdom you must abandon self-effort and tap into God's provision daily and moment by moment. Jesus said in John 15:5, "Without Me you can do nothing." Paul commanded Timothy to be strong in God's grace because it takes supernatural strength to do supernatural works. Timothy is to let God's grace give him the strength he needs. The challenge for every man is to live every day in total, complete dependence on God's grace and enabling power. How do you connect yourself to the grace of God? You abide in Him. Jesus said in John 15:4, "Abide in Me, and I in you. As the branch cannot bear fruit of itself, unless it abides in the vine, neither can you unless you abide in Me." The key to any spiritual endeavor is continual cooperation with God. Declare every day your dependence on Him. Say, "I can do all things through Christ who strengthens me" (Phil. 4:13).

The devil runs in fear when God's work is done by God's people in God's power. When men are empowered by God's mighty indwelling Spirit they are for certain a force to be reckoned with. Jesus said in Luke 10:19, "Behold, I have given you authority to tread on serpents and scorpions, and over all the power of the enemy, and nothing will injure you." God's grace is the blessing of His power. You are a passive recipient of His strength but you must actively submit to this power, surrender to it and yield to it. As a believer in Christ you have all you need inside of you. God is waiting for you to step out in faith so that signs and wonders will follow you wherever you go. When you tap into God's grace and power you'll be influential in the world you live in. You'll be a danger to the kingdom of darkness, a person the devil better not underestimate.

Your calling is to be a vessel in which God can pour His strength and power into. You prepare for war by allowing that to happen, by allowing His strength to become your strength. Paul said, "I will boast all the more gladly of my weaknesses so that the power of Christ may rest upon me" (2 Cor. 12:9). He is saying God's power can only be experienced in human weakness. This is why he said in vs. 10, "For when I am weak, then I am strong." AMP, "When I am weak in human strength, then am I truly strong, able, and powerful in divine strength." TPT, "My weakness becomes a portal to

God's power." Paul embraces his weaknesses viewing them as opportunities for God's power to be demonstrated in his life. He finds strength and satisfaction in his trials and hardships knowing that his weaknesses provides an opportunity for God's grace and power to be revealed in him and through him.

2 Cor. 4:7 (TPT) says, "We are like common clay jars that carry this glorious treasure within, so that this immeasurable power will be seen as God's, not ours." Hebrews 11 gives example after example of God working with people who "from weakness were made strong, became mighty in war, put foreign armies to flight" (vs. 34). The NLT says, "Their weakness was turned to strength." The Phillips Bible says, "From being weaklings they became strong men and mighty warriors; they routed whole armies of foreigners." Charles Spurgeon said, "They were quite as weak as the weakest of us, but by their faith they laid hold of heavenly strength until they could do all things. They achieved everything that was necessary in the form of service, and they bore up gloriously under the most fearful pressure of suffering simply and only by faith in God."

Strive daily to be like the saints of old who shook the powers of darkness with the irresistible power of weakness, the power that gives you the ability to do anything. All the kingdoms of Canaan were subdued by Joshua's faith as were the surrounding kingdoms of Moab, Syria, Edom, and many others by the faith of David. The faith of the three Hebrew children quenched the violence of fire, the faith of Daniel shut the mouths of lions, the faith of both Elijah and Elisha raised a person from the dead. Charles Spurgeon also said, "There was nothing in the range of possibility, or, I might say, nothing within the lines of impossibility, that they could not have performed." These heroes of faith accomplished all their great exploits with a power that was not their own. They were not naturally or spiritually strong in and of themselves.

If they had been, they would not have required faith in God. They needed to trust in Him and this they did. This is why their names are recorded to be examples for us to follow. Like them, you can have all unimaginable strength for the grandest achievements desirable if you will only have faith in God. Believe that when you are weak, then are you strong. If you feel weak and incapable of doing great things for God on the earth, then throw yourself on the infinite capacity of God. In faith let His strength become your strength. Do that and the sky is the limit of all that you can achieve. You'll be like those "who through faith subdued kingdoms, worked righteousness, obtained promises" (Heb. 11:33). Rise up and prepare for war. The Bible says that in faith you'll become mighty in war. Charles Spurgeon said, "When faith takes to working, how mighty she works."

| 7 |

"KEEP ON FIGHTING"

If you want to do mighty things with your life, then you must understand that self-discipline is a key to usefulness in the kingdom of God. This is a major battle we are in and the stakes couldn't be higher. The eternal souls of millions of people are weighing in the balance. This is why the world needs men who will prepare for war and wake up. It needs men who are trained, fit, and ready to enter into warfare. Indeed, there is a desperate need for disciplined soldiers to combat the enemy and make a lasting impact on the world for Christ. Ability will be of little value to you if you don't have the discipline to use it properly. Paul said in 1 Cor. 9:27, "I keep my body in complete submission to my spirit. If I don't do this, I am likely to be counted as one who did a lot of talking but finished up with the crowd." You must be disciplined if you want to be a good soldier in the Lord's army. 1 Tim. 4:7 (NASB) says, "Discipline yourself for the purpose of godliness." The NLT says to "train yourself to be godly."

Make no mistake about it, discipline is hard work. It doesn't happen on its own. The Greek word for "discipline" is where the English word "gymnasium" comes from. You go to the gym to work out. You push yourself to the limit as sweat drips off your face. Do the same thing, and more so, when it comes to spiritual discipline. Be disciplined in how you study the Word of God and in how you pray. Put all your heart into it. Ps. 62:8 says, "Trust in Him at all times, you people; Pour out your heart before Him." It takes hard work and discipline to be godly but it's worth all the effort you put into it. 1 Tim. 4:8 says, "For bodily exercise profits a little, but godliness is profitable for all things." Godliness is profitable in this life and in the life to come. It lasts for all eternity. Don't get hung up on how you look on the outside, focus on how you look on the inside.

There is a lasting, eternal impact that disciplined soldiers make on the world. You will make a positive difference when you're faithful to the Lord and faithful to speak the truth of God's Word. 1 Tim. 4:6 says, "If you instruct the brethren in these things, you will be a good minister of Jesus Christ." To be a good soldier, you must pass on what you've learned to others. Be disciplined to immerse yourself in the truth so you'll know the truth. A good soldier must be fit for battle. You prepare for war by eating solid food from the Word of God. Heb. 5:14 (NLT) says, "Solid food is for those who are mature, who through training have the skill to recognize the difference between right and wrong." Once you know the truth, you can share it with others. Wake up and prepare for war! Be a watchman on the wall! Sound the alarm! Speak the truth in love! Preach Jesus Christ and Him crucified!

A courageous soldier speaks the truth with authority, power, and conviction. They make things crystal clear. When the spotlight is in your face, tell people it's Jesus who sets people free. Acts 4:12 says, "Nor is there salvation in any other, for there is no other name under heaven given among men by which we must be saved." That is the message good soldiers are called to proclaim, not just with words but with our actions also. Prepare for war! Wake up and be an example for others to follow. 1 Tim. 4:12 (NLT) says, "Be an example to all believers in what you say, in the way you live, in your love, your faith, and your purity." You will make a difference when you are faithful to live out the truth in your life. James 1:22 says, "But be doers of the word, and not hearers only, deceiving ourselves."

There's an old saying that says, "Your life speaks so loudly that I can't hear what you say." It's true, your actions speak louder than your words. You've got to walk the walk and not just talk the talk. People would rather see a sermon than hear one any day. Good advice is often confusing but an example is always clear. Thomas Fuller once said, "Teaching is putting nails in the wood, an example is hammering them in deeply." People are watching you. They watch what you do and listen to what you say. Be a good example to them. Let your light shine. Walk the walk. Be like Paul who said, "Imitate me, just as I also imitate Christ" (1 Cor. 11:1). Say to others, "Follow my example. Do what I'm doing." Be disciplined and make a positive difference in this evil world. That's what being a good soldier is all about.

To be a good soldier, you have to be disciplined and you have to have courage. Sissies and wimps don't make good soldiers and are not to be found in the Lord's army. In fact, Rev. 21:8 says the cowardly will be the first group of people who "shall have their part in the lake of fire that burns with fire and brimstone." The Greek word for "cowardly" is "deilois" and it refers to 'people showing fear in a shameful way.' This word is used to describe a lack of faith (Matt. 8:26). The wicked and lazy servant hid his talent in the ground out of fear rather than investing it for the Lord's benefit. He was cast into outer darkness (Matt. 25:25). Many of the religious rulers believed in Jesus but for fear of being put out of the synagogue would not confess Him. They loved the praise of men more than the praise of God (John 12:43).

Winston Churchill said, "Courage is the most important of the virtues because it is the one virtue that makes all others possible." Being a coward is an abomination because 2 Tim. 1:7 says, "For God has not given us a spirit of fear, but of power and of love and of a sound mind." The GWT says, "God didn't give us a cowardly spirit but a spirit of power, love, and good judgment." The Holy Spirit empowers you with strength and the ability to discipline yourself. God's nature is to give you a spirit of confidence and trust. Micah 3:8 says, "I am filled with power, with the Spirit of the Lord, and with justice and courage." Before His ascension into heaven the Lord said to His disciples, "You are to stay in the city until you are clothed with power from on high" (Luke 24:49).

You are a warrior in the Lord's army. In Him you are strong and mighty, bold and confident. Without a doubt there is no room for cowardice in good soldiers who fight. There is no retreat in the Lord's army. At one time the motto of the French Foreign Legion declared, "If I falter, push me on. If I stumble, pick me up. If I retreat, shoot me." Every man of God is in a war! The devil is forever seeking to devour you, your family, and everything and everything that is important to you. Neh. 4:14 (NLT), "Don't be afraid of the enemy! Remember the Lord, who is great and glorious, and fight for your brothers, your sons, your daughters, your wives, and your homes!" This is why you must wake up every day and prepare for war. Fight on! Fight on! Fight on! What good is having a nice house if the home inside it is crumbling?

Courageous soldiers know that boldness has consequences. Not everybody will like it when you speak boldly and openly about the Lord. The Sadducees were greatly disturbed and furious that the people were being taught by Peter and John that in Jesus there is a resurrection from the dead (Acts 4:1,2). So enraged were these religious leaders that Peter and John were thrown into jail for what they preached. This story shows it takes courage and boldness to stand up for the truth of God's Word. Yes, there are consequences for standing up for what's right. This is why there is no place for cowards in the Lord's army. Never fear the enemy. "If God be for us, who can be against us" (Rom. 8:31). Never let intimidation stop you from going to war. 1 Peter 3:14 (NLT), "But even if you suffer for doing what is right, God will reward you for it. So don't worry or be afraid of their threats."

How do you prepare for war? James 4:7 says, "Summit your-selves therefore to God. Resist the devil, and he will flee from you." The weapon to use in a declaration of war is to submit to God. Complete and total submission to God is the first weapon of the mighty man. To win this battle of life you must surrender your will to God's will. This is what gives you the power and strength to resist the devil. It allows you to reap the benefit of watching him flee from your life. Submit to God and put on the armor of God. Put on truth, righteousness, the gospel of peace, faith, salvation (Eph. 6:13-17). Learn these virtues well. Know them inside out. As a man you must know how to speak the truth in love and live righteously. You must be forever ready to spread the good news that gives peace. Most important of all, you must live a life of faith. You must cling to your salvation and work it out daily in your life, and you must pray and submit to God at all times.

You only have the ability to resist the enemy to the degree that you're submitted to God. You have to keep on fighting. You fight to get to the top and then you fight to stay on the top. Don't run from the battle. Submit to God, resist the devil, and keep on fighting. As long as there is breath in your body, you will always be fighting. Luke 4:13 (NLT), "When the devil had finished tempting Jesus, he left him until the next opportunity came." The devil is relentless in his attacks. Don't confuse a "let up" with a "give up." In the wilderness Jesus resisted the devil three times. If you want Satan to leave you alone for a season then like Jesus, you must constantly resist him. Many are attacked because they resist so little. The devil will leave you for a season but, make no mistake about it, he's coming back. He'll back away for a little while but will come back at a more opportune time.

In the Garden of Gethsemane he tempted Jesus more severely than he did in the wilderness. He was trying to get Jesus to pull back from going to the cross with all its agony and horror. He knows when you're strong and when you're not. He'll wait until you're tired and weary, when you've let your guard down a little bit. This can often happen after you've scored a victory over his attempts to take you down. You are often the most vulnerable when you think you are the least vulnerable. Make no mistake about it, the devil is always lurking in the background, forever ready like a bird of prey to suddenly swoop down and destroy your life (Gen. 4:7). Constant vigilance is required. As a man of war you can never relax your guard until you meet Jesus face to face. You must be as watchful after a victory as you were before the battle began.

You are a soldier in the army of the Lord and fighting is what you do. The good news is you'll win these battles if you don't give up the fight and quit. Winners never quit and quitters never win. Jesus said, "The gates of hell will not prevail against the church" (Matt. 16:18). The Message Bible tells of "a church so expansive with energy that not even the gates of hell will be able to keep it out." We'll win if we remain firm in our commitment to be true to the commands of God despite temptation, opposition, and adversity. You must choose your battles wisely. There are some things not worth fighting over. Don't waste your time fighting a battle that has no spoils. In some victories you lose more than you gain so choose wisely. You may win an argument with your wife but lose your fellowship with her and the respect she had for you. If winning a battle causes you to lose your peace, then your victory is too expensive.

Know also that your identity is often formed by what you struggle with. People who struggle with alcohol are called alcoholics. If you struggle with infidelity, then you are identified as an unfaithful person. You then live out this sinful nature because you've been identified with infidelity. Your struggle becomes your identity. This is why you need to wrestle with God. Jacob wrestled with God and his name was changed to "Israel" which means 'one who struggles with God' (Gen. 32). If you'll struggle with Him, you'll get a God-identity. It happened to Jacob, and it can happen to you. David struggled with Goliath and received the identity of a giant-killer. Don't get your identity in your abilities, get your identity in what God will do for you. David said, "The Lord who rescued me from the paw of the lion and the paw of the bear will rescue me from the hand of this Philistine" (1 Sam. 17:37).

Spiritual warfare is the cosmic war of good vs. evil. It's a daily battle between the kingdom of God and the world system ruled by the devil. God's kingdom is a kingdom of love, trust, fulfillment, and generosity. Satan's kingdom is a kingdom of hate, suspicion, frustration, and greed. God's kingdom is a kingdom of clarity, obedience, freedom, and wellness. Satan's kingdom is a kingdom of confusion, rebellion, bondage, and sickness. God's kingdom is a kingdom of harmony, creativity, purpose, and peace. Satan's kingdom is a kingdom of discord, imitation, aimless pleasure, and anxiety. There is a war raging between two kingdoms in conflict, and you are in that war. What should you do? Prepare for war and wake up. Be ready for battle at all times.

How do you win the spiritual battle? Your first response to spiritual warfare is resistance. It's what allows you to stand firm against all the strategies of the devil. The only way to resist unseen evil spiritual forces is to continually rely on the power of God. Trust Him and you'll receive supernatural power to stand your ground against the enemy. Eph. 6:13 (NLT) says, "Therefore, put on every piece of God's armor so you will be able to resist the enemy in the time of evil." There is no warfare when you give in to the schemes of the devil. There is only warfare when there is resistance. Men lose the battle when they refuse to resist the enemy. To be successful, you must resist everything that is not a part of God's plan and purpose for your life. The power to resist is God's but the choice to resist is yours. Do not fear the enemy but choose to face him head on. Cowardice never wins against Satan, only faith and courage.

Put your shield up so all the fiery darts of the enemy bounce away from you. A shield is for resistance. Spiritual warfare is all about resisting the devil. James 4:7 says, "Therefore submit to God. Resist the devil and he will flee from you." You only have the power to resist the devil to the degree that you are submitted to God. You have no strength, no power, and no authority to resist the devil when you have not submitted yourself to God. You will need the power of God to keep the devil out of your life and out of your home. The devil is always trying to get inside your life and the lives of your family. He wants to become a part of all of you. He knows he can accomplish more through infiltration than through confrontation. This is why he wants to get into the homes, churches, schools, and organizations of all men. It's through infiltration that the devil does the most damage.

He'll come as an angel of light to get you to think he's the real deal. Submit to God and let the Holy Spirit be your Counselor. Let Him reveal to you the wicked and deceitful schemes of the enemy. The devil will try to derail your walk with the Lord but the Holy Spirit is there to warn you and guide you. The devil is very subtle but the Holy Spirit knows what he's up to. Stay connected to the Holy Spirit in every area of warfare. Rom. 8:26 (AMP) says, "The Spirit comes to us and helps us in our weaknesses." A. T. Robertson said, "The Holy Spirit lays hold of our weaknesses along with us and carries His part of the burden facing us as if two men were carrying a log, one at each end." TPT, "The Holy Spirit takes hold of us in our human frailty to empower us in our weakness." No wonder Paul said, "When I am weak, then am I strong" (2 Cor. 12:9).

| 8 |

"WAR MENTALITY"

Eccl. 3:1,8 (NLT) says, "For everything there is a season, a time for every activity under heaven. A time to love and a time to hate. A time for war and a time for peace." Seasons come and go in our life and we need the wisdom of God to know what to do and how to act in whatever season we may be in. Discernment is absolutely necessary to know when one season has ended and a new season has begun. Wisdom is doing the right thing in the right season with the right people. It takes wisdom to know when a season has shifted, when a season has changed. You've got to know what season you're in. Why? Because you do different things in different seasons. Joel 3:9, "Prepare for war! Wake up the mighty men. Let all the men of war draw near. Let them come up." Joel is saying to the people it is now the season of war.

In vs.10 he tells the people to turn their farming equipment into weapons of war, "Beat your plowshares into swords and your pruninghooks into spears. Let the weak say, 'I am strong.'" This is a rallying cry, a call to arms, a call to prepare for confrontation, a summons to engage in active hostilities, a call to defend against a takeover. The battle against evil is the war of all wars. All men are to equip themselves for battle and boldly march into the camp of those who war against the people of God. This is a holy war and even those who are weak are to stir themselves up to be a warrior as is generally the case when a whole nation is seized with warlike enthusiasm. Stiffen up your courage and proclaim for all to hear, "I am a mighty man!" Even those who are weak will be a force to be reckoned with on the day of battle.

2 Sam. 11:1 tells of "the time when kings go forth to battle." There are times when all men who are kings unto God (Rev. 1:6) should go forth to battle in a special and spectacular way. Indeed, every day is a day of battle and all men should be active in this ongoing war. There should never be an idle day, or a wasted hour, or a barren moment with a warrior of God. Shake off the dust of idleness and go forth into battle. Grab hold of your calling knowing that God will always furnish all His servants with plenty of work to do. If nothing else, you can always pray. Oh, what strength the body of Christ gets from men who pray, men who bring down the divine lightning from heaven to the earth. There is nothing more strengthening for the feeble and weak then to gird himself to do something for his Lord and Master. If you will but put forth the effort, God will surely help you.

If you will use what little ability you have, you shall have more. The one talent will become two, the two will become four, and the four shall multiply over and over again. The devil does not rest and neither should you. Always be on your guard. Stand firm in the faith. If you waver in being prepared the devil will surely pounce on you. Life is a struggle so devote yourself to the preparation of war. Arm yourself with the determination and drive to fight knowing God will lead you to triumph in Christ Jesus (2 Cor. 2:14). Is. 25:4 says, "For You have been a strength to the poor, a strength to the needy in his distress, a refuge from the storm, a shade from the heat." Ps. 5:11,12 says, "But let all those rejoice who put their trust in You; Let them ever shout for joy, because You defend them. With favor You will surround him as with a shield."

The devil has unleashed a diabolical attack on the church and the mighty men of God must prepare for war! You will miss God if you have a farming mentality when you should have a war mentality. It is now time to be warriors, not farmers. You must arm and prepare yourself for battle. Put away those golf clubs and fishing pole. It's time to prepare for war. It's time to rebuke the wind and the waves. It's time to rebuke the works of the enemy. It's time to rebuke sickness and disease, poverty and debt, sin and evil, divorce and separation. Shout the war cry! It's time to go to war! It's time to tell the devil, "Not on my watch!" It's time for courage to rise up in the hearts of men. It's time for men to say, "I was made for this!" With discernment you'll understand the time and you'll know what to do.1 Chron. 12:22 says there "were men that had understanding of the times, to know what Israel ought to do."

You are a spiritual soldier in a spiritual battle and if ever there was a time when God's people are called to take up arms and go to war it is now. The call to arms has gone forth and it is to you that the summons to war has come. Now is the time to wake up, arise, and go forth like kings to the battle. The world is covered with thick darkness and your calling is to shine brightly and burn with the fire of the Spirit of God that is deep inside of you. Follow the impulse in your inner man to break loose from the worldly ties and those things of the flesh that will entangle you and hinder your service to God. You are here for a specific purpose. You are here to be the devil's worst nightmare. Go forth into battle and dedicate yourself to bringing glory and honor to your King.

An alarm is going off in the realm of the Spirit. It's time to wake up the mighty men of God. Why? Because it's time for war! Mighty men know what time it is and what needs to be done. The kingdom of God does not advance in the world without war, without passion, and without good soldiers. The world desperately needs strong men who will stand up and fight, men who prepare for war. Do not excuse yourself from battle because you think you are weak. It is not in the strength you have that wins the battle, it's the strength God gives you as you need it (Is. 40:30,31). Unfortunately, there is an assault on manhood in the world today, a satanic attack on how real men are supposed to live and act. It's happening because what Satan fears most, he attacks the hardest. Many men have lost their way. They've been feminized and don't do the things real men are supposed to do. They act like they were made in the image of Satan and not in the image of God.

Being a man is not about who you think you are of even who you want to be. It's about you looking unto the God who made you and the purpose He brought you into existence. God did not make you to sit in your mother's basement and play video games all day. He made you to be a mighty warrior and to rise up and fight the good fight of faith. Just know that what the devil attacks ferociously is a sign of what it is that will take him down. If you want to know what the enemy fears, look at where he puts his most effort. We live in a world that celebrates feminine men and crucifies warriors. It is this war that the mighty men of God enter into battle, a war they are commissioned to win. There is a war to be fought and a work to be done so what are you waiting for? Take the bread and the fish in your hand and go forth and feed the thousands of people before you.

Not only is this an attack on men, it's an attack on the power and might inside of a man. Evil thrives on weakness. A man who is oppressed and defeated is a weak man, a man who has laid his weapons down. He's a man who has given up, a man with no power and might, a man who has fallen asleep. That's the man the devil runs rampant over. This is why it's time to wake up the mighty man. What makes mighty men mighty? Battle! Mighty men are defined by resistance, by battle, by war. It's in the storms of life where mighty men are revealed. It's where they strive. A strong man excels in battle. He always bounces back from setbacks and challenges, learning from adversity and using it as a catalyst for growth. Hard times create strong men. A real man doesn't ignore his problems or blame them on someone else. No, he takes responsibility and embraces ownership of every aspect of his life.

He has a strong sense of purpose and direction in life, striving daily to make a positive impact in the world. He treats others with respect regardless of their status in life. A man's strength encompasses qualities like emotional resilience, integrity, and a strong sense of purpose. He navigates life with a commitment to fulfilling his God-given destiny. Mighty men get stronger when trouble comes. They don't cry when hard times come because it's hard times that make them mighty. They don't bend and break and never bow down to wickedness. The devil hates it when men realize that in Christ they are stronger than he is. This is why he strives to keep you ignorant to the power that resides inside of you. At the same time, he hates men who refuse to tremble in fear. He knows resistance is your finest hour. The devil is under your feet so don't fear him. Instead, resist him at all times.

David was the king over the entire nation of Israel. He was a very prominent man and was the commander of a large army. He had thousands of soldiers who served him faithfully. Among this huge army, scripture records that David had three mighty men who stood out among all the rest. They were warriors who were ready to go to war at his command. These three men were in David's inner circle. He knew them personally and had a close relationship with them. They were mightier and stronger than the common, average man. They were feared and highly regarded by other men. The chief among David's mighty men was Adino the Eznite. One day in battle he killed 800 men by himself (2 Sam. 23:8). The second mighty man was Eleazar. He helped David defeat the Philistines when the rest of the men of Israel had retreated (vs. 9). He fought so long and hard that his hand stuck to his sword.

The third mighty man was Shammah. The enemy came to steal the crops of Israel but Shammah stood in a field of lentils all by himself, defended it, and killed the Philistines (vs. 11,12). Mighty men put themselves in harm's way for it's an opportunity to go from ordinary to extraordinary, from mediocre to mighty. It's battle that reveals what a real man is made of. The battles we fight are God-given opportunities to become great. Seize the opportunity. Be a mighty man and take the battle to the enemy. Don't run from the devil, make him run from you. Doors of opportunity will be opened to you but you must have the courage to walk through them. God does not use mediocre men, those who are satisfied with the mundane. God is looking for mighty men, men who shun mediocrity and are willing to go on to greatness, men who are willing to fight for the glory and honor of the King they serve.

In the garden of Gethsemane, Jesus rebuked His disciples for sleeping when they should have been awake keeping watch with Him (Matt. 26:40-45). This was a very intense moment in the life of Jesus and yet His disciples were asleep. He probably wanted to kick them and say, "Wake up you bunch of mediocre men!" The problem today is too many men have convinced themselves that God accepts mediocrity. No, He does not! Many men today are sleeping because they think all is well when in fact it isn't well at all. They deceive themselves into thinking God accepts casual, loose, mediocre manhood. They think they serve a permissive God that demands nothing and expects nothing out of them. Nothing could be farther from the truth. This is a false revelation of who God is and what he expects. This is why Joel 3:9 says, "Prepare for war! Wake up the mighty men!"

To be a mighty man you must deny yourself, take up your cross, and follow Him. You must be willing to give up your life for His sake. To become mighty you must take yourself out of the equation. Lay your pride to the side. Surrender your heart to God. Put His will above your own. David was a mighty man not because of all the battles he won but because he was a man after God's own heart. You serve a God who demands greatness! Not average. Not mediocre. Greatness! Greatness is not about how good you feel, it's about putting God above all else that is in your life. He expects you to reflect His character through humility, service, and living according to His will, ultimately achieving a greatness that is defined by His holy standards. Trust God, walk in His ways, and you will be great. Ps. 71: 21 says, "You shall increase my greatness, and comfort me on every side." MSG, "You made me stare trouble in the face."

Don't be afraid of the devil, be afraid of falling asleep. Be afraid of napping on your watch. Your greatest enemy isn't the devil; it's sleep and laziness and apathy. It's a lack of interest, enthusiasm, and concern for the things of God. Your greatest enemy is to waste the precious time God has given you to accomplish His purpose on the earth. Rom. 13:12 (TPT) says, "Night's darkness is dissolving away as a new day of destiny dawns." In other words, it's time for the mighty men of God to prepare for war and wake up. The end is near and Charles Spurgeon said, "The fact that Jesus Christ is to come again is not a reason for star gazing, but for working in the power of the Holy Ghost." It is time for war and all the men of God need to rise up off the bed of slumber. They need to wake up from a state of inactivity, lethargy, and spiritual complacency.

Rom. 13:11 says, "It is time for you to wake up from your sleep" and Eph. 5:14 says, "Awake, you who sleep, arise from the dead, and Christ will give you light." There is a raging war going on and it's time to wake up and get up. Is. 60:1 says, "Arise, shine, for your light has come, and the glory of the Lord has risen upon you." The enemy is using a worldwide assault to consume our world with darkness. What you see in the natural realm is just a reflection of what is happening in the spiritual realm. The devil wants to crush all the power and might that is in it. He wants to stop the one thing that can stop him. He wants to stop the mighty man of God. If Jesus is your Lord and Savior then daily your life should be a manifestation of His marvelous light. Eph. 5:8 says, "You are light in the Lord. Walk as children of light."

The darker the night gets, the brighter your Spirit-empowered light should shine. Let your light be the dawn of a new day, a day of "peace on earth, good will toward men" (Luke 2:14). The only thing standing between darkness and the world are the mighty men of God. It's time to have the shield of faith in one hand and the sword of the Spirit in the other. Decide to stop being pushed around by the enemy. Wake up and realize God is with you. Make up your mind to fulfill the will of God. There is nothing more powerful than a made-up mind. Stop running from the voice of God. The world needs you to answer the call to be mighty. Grit your teeth and say, "I can do what God has called me to do." Allow your actions to preach a sermon wherever you go. Use the light you're walking in to diminish the darkness that surrounds those not yet surrendered to Christ.

There is a call on your life to change the world and God uses this call to be the alarm clock that wakes you up. Rise up and respond in the power that the call created. Mighty men are not born, they're formed. Gideon was defeated and hiding from the enemy when the Lord appeared and called him a mighty man of valor (Judges 6:12). The Lord then said, "Go in this might of yours, and you shall save Israel from the hand of the Midianites" (vs. 14). Greatness is not in your genes; it's in the decision you make to be who God called you to be. God said in vs. 16, 'Surely I will be with you, and you shall defeat Midian as one man." He is calling Gideon to go forward with the supplied strength that always accompanies the divine call. Gideon's call comes directly from the Lord. He is left with no doubt about either his duty or his success. He knows victory comes when your confidence is in God and not yourself.

| 9 |

"SLEEPING GIANTS"

Napoleon once pointed to a map of China and said, "There lies a sleeping giant. If it ever wakes up, it will be unstoppable." Sad to say, many men today are sleeping giants. A man who is a sleeping giant has powerful potential to bring about positive change in the world but it is currently untapped, dormant, and underutilized. Underutilized implies that a man has the capacity to be used more effectively for a greater purpose but his sleepiness leads to decreased productivity and missed opportunities. Inside of these men is immense power which they possess through faith, prayer, and action but, sad to say, they are spiritually asleep and currently inactive and unengaged. Your potential is referred to as a giant. Indeed, it is vast, massive, and colossal. When used for the glory of God great things are achieved and the world becomes a better place.

All men have great talents and abilities and the church would explode with massive growth if the potential of every man was poured out into the lives of others. When Paul told Timothy "to stir up the gift of God which is in you" (2 Tim. 1:6) he was telling him to wake up the sleeping giant, to keep constantly ablaze the gift of God. John MacArthur said, "The product of sincere faith is faithful service, and the heart of faithful service is ministering our gift what God distributes "to each one individually just as He wills" (1 Cor. 12:11). Inside of you is the power to make the impossible possible. The giant of greatness is inside of you and you must wake him up. Your greatness must be realized and the power must be attained. God is a God of power and might. Wake up and put on strength and dignity. Activate the giant in you and then go out into the world and be a mighty force to be reckoned with.

The call of God is on the life of every man and yet many of them are asleep. Too many men live lives of quiet desperation and go to the grave with their potential still in them. If the enemy is ever to be defeated, then all the mighty men in the church need to wake up. This is a time for battle, a time of war. Men, it's time to wake up the sleeping giant and fulfill your destiny. Charles Spurgeon said, "God deserves to be served with all the energy of which we are capable." Theologian Samuel Chadwick said, "Men ablaze are invincible. Hell trembles when men kindle." Anyone who has prepared a campfire for warmth or cooking is fully aware that the coals need to be stirred up occasionally. As long as they are glowing, they can be stirred into a raging fire. The Greek word for "stir up" is "anazopureo" and it means 'to keep in full flame, kindle afresh, stir up the fire, reactivate, cause to begin to be active again.'

Stirring up your gift and waking up the sleeping giant is a progressive, continuous action. Keep kindling the gift inside of you. Make it your aim to continually keep it at full flame. What is a fire made for but to burn? Paul was telling Timothy to blow the coals into a burning flame, to shake the ashes off the God-given fire that was in him. Every fire needs repeated stirring to keep it burning brightly. Do not let your zeal in the great cause for which you've been set apart become smoldering ashes and not a dancing fire. You can't be passive and expect the effects of your spiritual gift to just happen. Keep fanning the coals that are already burning. it's your responsibility to rekindle your spiritual gift. God's gifts must be used if they are to reach and maintain their full potential. Like China, if you will wake up the sleeping giant you also will be unstoppable.

The missing man has become the major crisis in today's world and one of the dominate questions in the Bible is found in Gen. 3:9 when God asked Adam, "Where are you?" Most single women can't find a worthwhile man to marry. They're calling out, "Where are you?" The abandoned mother and child are asking the man who left them, "Where are you?" God is asking the same question, "Where are you?" Don't leave this world with unfulfilled potential, with gifts never developed, with services never rendered to God. Wake up because within you are enormous gifts, abilities, and talents that you have yet to discover. Don't go to the grave with abilities still locked inside you, with gifts never developed and used. Don't go to the grave with books never written, with prayers never prayed, with songs never composed, with leadership never developed.

It's time to wake up and discover all the wonderful gifts and talents God has placed within you. It's time to stop running away from your responsibilities and be the man God created you to be. In the Garden of Eden, Adam abandoned his position as leader of the family and caretaker of his home. The desperate need of the day is to call males back to being men. Not just any man, but what God calls a man. One of the first things we learn about being a man of God is that he is in a position of priority. 1 Tim. 2:13 says, "For Adam was formed first, then Eve." The word "first" has to do with order, with progress in time. It's important to know that Adam and Eve were not created at the same time. Adam was created first, then Eve. God spends an entire chapter, Genesis 2, discussing things with Adam before Eve was even created. Why? Because it would be the man who would be responsible for the family.

God created Adam first because God would hold him responsible. Adam and Eve both sinned and hid from God. When God came looking for them He didn't say, "Adam and Eve, where are you?" No, He said, "Adam, where are you?" He addressed Adam because it was Adam who was responsible for what happened. The burden of responsibility was his and his alone. In the Bible, God asks over three thousand questions but none is more relevant than the one He asks every man, "Where are you?" This question is not for God, it's for you. God addressed Adam personally and He is doing the same to you. God wants you to know where you are. He wants you to ask the question, "Where am I? Am I where God wants me to be?" He is interested in you as an individual, as a born again believer, and, most prominent, as a man. He wants you to know where you are intellectually, morally, and spiritually.

Be a man and face where you are head on. Don't run off and hide behind some tree like Adam did. He and his wife hid their nakedness from each other and they both hid themselves from God. Adam was ashamed of his failure and broken relationship. The source of that shame came from knowing he had violated his responsibility to fulfill his role as a man. Don't let this happen to you. If you're going to be a mighty man of God, you're going to have to accept responsibility for the things God has put under your care. Because man was created first, he is to function as the foundation of the home. If the foundation crumbles, everything on top of it will crumble also. The missing man is the biggest crisis of our day. Not the missing male, the missing man. Examine the spiritual condition of your heart and ask yourself, "Am I being the man God wants me to be?"

Gen. 2:15 says, "Then the Lord God took the man and put him in the garden of Eden to cultivate it and keep it." The CSB says he was put there "to work it and watch over it." Notice that God gave Adam work before pleasure and this happened before the fall. Even in paradise man had to work revealing that no man is put into the world to be idle. God was telling Adam to be productive where He put him, to put forth vigilance to ensure growth and well-being. To "cultivate" means to produce something more than what you started with. In the parable of the talents, the two faithful servants doubled what their master had given them. God expects a man to maximize his potential in whatever sphere of opportunity God gives him. To cultivate what God has given you emphasizes the importance of stewardship. It is your responsibility to care for your own spiritual life, your family, and the community you live in.

God wants you to nurture faith, to grow in knowledge, and to develop godly virtues. Do that and you'll be well equipped to go out and help make this world a better place. God also told Adam to keep the garden where he lived. The word "keep" means to guard and protect. God wanted Adam to protect his home, to keep the garden safe from all intruders. The Hebrew word "shamar" was used to describe a shepherd keeping watch over a flock of sheep. It means 'to watch carefully over, to be on one's guard.' Just as there was a serpent in the garden, so also will there be problems and temptations in your home. Your job is to keep the serpent out of your home. It is your responsibility to keep the devil away from your family. Don't be ignorant of the fact that the enemy is trying to get into your life and the lives of your loved ones.

The call of God on your life is to storm the gates of hell, to strike fear in the heart of your enemy. Just know that you can't defeat the enemy if all you do is wile away the hours conferring with the flowers. You can't win if all you do is tiptoe through the tulips. To win you must wake up, rise, up, and fight like never before. You are a warrior in God's army and a pioneering spirit is inside you. You are unstoppable and you're to terrorize the opposition. Don't fear the devil, make him fear you. What would the world look like if every Christian man felt this way, if every man had the passion to go to war? For sure, the last thing the devil wants is for you to wake up. Mighty men are spiritual leaders. They have an ever-growing relationship with God that turns them into role models that others can follow. David wrote in Ps. 101:2, "I will behave wisely in a perfect way. I will walk within my house with a perfect heart." Character matters. Joseph lost his coat of many colors and his freedom, but he never lost his character.

Because of that, God lifted him up beyond his wildest dreams. In the end, character is what matters most. It's what turns you into a mighty man of valor. Billy Graham once said, "When wealth is lost, nothing is lost. When health is lost, something is lost. When character is lost, everything is lost." The truth is, when mighty men with character wake up the church will experience its finest hour. This is why the devil is doing everything he can to silence the mighty men of God. If a child comes to Christ, 3% of the families will follow. If a woman comes to Christ, 17% follow. But if a man comes to Christ, 93% of families follow. If you get the man, you get the family. Too many men want the title of being the head of the home without the responsibility that goes with it. Be like Joshua who said, "As for me and my house, we will serve the Lord" (Josh. 24:15).

There is so much social confusion in the world today that a lot of men don't know who or what they're supposed to be. Outcries of equality cause women to act like men and men to act like women. To make matters worse, the media feeds this crossing over of roles. They make movies where men act dumb and stupid while the woman is the hero who saves the day. Instead of fighting against all this, most men go hide in a cave and fall asleep. Samson got his hair cut off and lost his strength when he fell asleep in the lap of Delilah. Instead of preparing for war, men go play golf all day and tune out what is happening around them. Or else they become workaholics and don't have time for God, their family, and their church. In other words, they've fallen asleep and are not doing what needs to be done. Families and churches and nations become dysfunctional when men refuse to take on the role they've been called to fulfill.

It's true, evil prevails when good men do nothing. This is why we must sound the alarm, "Prepare for war! Wake up the mighty men! Let all the men of war draw near. Let them come up." And then there are those described in Dan. 11:32, "The people who know their God shall be strong and carry out great exploits." The NASB says they will "display strength and take action." This verse is saying those who remain steadfast in their faith and are forever loyal to God, even in the face of persecution, will demonstrate toughness and resilience. This is a great promise and one of the most courageous verses in all the Bible. To do great exploits you must first have an intimate relationship with God. Knowing God is more than knowing about God. People who know God spend quality time with Him and they know His power works with them.

Charles Spurgeon said, "Every believer understands that to know God is the highest and best form of knowledge, and this spiritual knowledge is a source of strength to the Christian." He said, "Knowledge strengthens love, as well as faith. Knowledge opens the door and then through that door we see our Savior. We cannot love a Christ we do not know." The knowledge of God, combined with the strength that comes from God, is the most powerful and persistent force against evil in this dark world. Ex. 15:3 says, "The Lord is a man of war; The Lord is His name." Those men who enlist in God's army have a Commander who will train them for the conflict and give them both strength and valor. In ancient times, it was believed that a god's strength was reflected in the strength of his people. If one nation defeated another nation, it was clear that their god was obviously greater.

God also wants His people to be strong and do great things so that others might recognize that He alone is the one true God. He wants it known that nothing is greater than His strength. David said to Goliath, "This day the Lord will deliver you into my hand, and I will strike you and take your head from you so that all the earth may know there is a God in Israel (1 Sam. 17:46). You may be a physical giant on the outside but a spiritual wimp on the inside. Goliath was over nine feet tall but he was killed by a teenager who knew the God of Israel. God wants you to wake up and do bold and courageous actions in His name. These exploits are dynamic acts of faith and obedience that demonstrate God's power and glory. God is looking for men through whom He can display His extraordinary power. He wants all men to do mighty deeds that bear witness to the reality of who He is.

God is raising up men who will know Him intimately, men who will be transformed into His image, men who will do great exploits for the glory of His name. God wants you to be a willing vessel to be used by Him here in the last days. He wants to use you to reveal His glory and power to a dying world. God wants to do mighty things through your life. He wants you to rise up and do heroic acts of daring exploits. The word "exploit" refers to an adventurous or heroic act in the face of difficulty or opposition. The Bible is full of stories of the great exploits of men who knew God and trusted Him. Gideon was an unlikely hero but he and his 300 men defeated the 135,000 man Midianite army. Gideon's story highlights God's ability to use seemingly weak individuals to achieve great things. It reveals to all of us how God can strengthen men who are willing to trust Him.

Heb. 11:34 (AMP) says there are those who "out of weakness were made strong, became mighty and unbeatable, putting enemy forces to flight." TPT, "Although weak, their faith imparted power to make them strong! Faith sparked courage within them and they became mighty warriors in battle." Jesus said in John 14:12, "Greater works than these shall you do because I go to the Father." Let these words burn inside of you. Dare to do great exploits with your life. Be satisfied with nothing less. Be willing to reach beyond the ordinary and do the extraordinary. The world needs to see a rise in deeds of heroism from men doing great exploits in the name of their God. Do great exploits for God with a boldness that comes from within. All mighty men must show courage and bravery and do significant feats that will change history and move people to action.

| 10 |

"MEN OF VALOR"

T oday there is an absence of real men in the church. Why? Because the enemy has robbed them of their desire to be great. In other words, he has lulled them to sleep. The devil doesn't have to devour you to make you ineffective. All he has to do is put you to sleep. If you're asleep, you'll never become the man God created you to be. An emptiness will always be inside of you. You'll never be satisfied and you'll never be fulfilled. Not all men are mighty men. A lot of men are tore up from the floor up. They've allowed the enemy to lull them to sleep thus making them ineffective in the world today. They may not be mighty now, but they can be. They can be transformed by the power of God. Rom. 12:2, "Don't copy the behavior and customs of this world, but let God transform you into a new person by changing the way you think. Then you will know what God wants you to do."

In the Bible, the word "transformation" means 'change or renewal from a life that no longer conforms to the ways of the world to one that pleases God.' You need to stop imitating the ideals and opinions of the world around you and be inwardly transformed by the Holy Spirit through a total reformation of how you think. This is accomplished by the renewing of your mind, by an inward spiritual transformation that will manifest itself in outward actions, in "bearing fruit in every good work" (Col. 1:10). 2 Chron. 16:0 says, "For the eyes of the Lord run to and fro throughout the whole earth, to show Himself strong on behalf of those whose heart is loyal to Him." God is looking for men who are not asleep like the rest of the world. He is looking for men who wake up and fight, men who win, men who conquer, men who overcome.

The church today is in desperate need of real men who look like Christ and act like Christ, men moved by the explosive power of a new affection for the things of God. It's looking for men to wake up from their slumber and become men of valor, men who have moral worth and won't let the circumstances of life defeat them. Men of valor are men of courage and fearlessness especially in battle. They have strength of mind and spirit that enables them to encounter danger with courage, firmness, and decisiveness. Men of valor are rare in a world that has lost it's moral compass. This is why you need to live with a clear conscience and a heart that lives victoriously through God for His glory. We are in a war for purity and righteousness, in a battle for our loved ones, in a conflict for the kingdom of God. To be a mighty man of valor you must be prepared to fight each and every day.

What is a man of valor? He's a man whose goodness, honesty, and strength of character lead him to defend what he believes in with certainty. He lives by the Spirit of God and seeks to glorify God. You can't be passive and be a mighty man. You must seek every day to maximize your development into full manhood with every ounce of energy that you have. You must fight against the spirit of feminism and homosexuality that is trying to womanize each and every man, to fight against the media's perception that all men are sissies and wimps. You must fight against the natural millennial desire for ease and comfort, against your own flesh that wants to cruise through life and not fight for things that are right and true. God needs men who will prepare for war and wake up, men who will stand up and show the world what being a man of valor is all about, men who will be the man God created him to be.

To be a man of valor you must push yourself to the utmost. You will not reach your full potential and make a difference in this world unless you work harder than everyone else. Men of valor are never satisfied with where they're at in their level of spiritual development. They want to go higher and farther, to exceed what they've previously done. Few men reach the full extent of their ability during the course of their lives. Science has shown that most men do not use more than 5% of their intellectual capacity. Why is this true? Because men have been asleep for way too long and now is the time for them to wake up because they have been given the grand opportunity to change the world. Real men are hard workers and they avoid comfortable situations. If easy things are all they do, they know they will soon become lazy, sluggish, and lethargic.

No, they put their hand to the plow and don't look back (Luke 9:62). It is difficult to plow a straight and narrow path if you are looking behind rather than forward. They set God-given goals for themselves to fulfill and once they begin the process to achieve those goals they never look back with regret and second thoughts. No, they press forward with dedication and focus. Plowing requires concentration and forward movement and looking back is a distraction that can potentially lead to failure. All men need to have a vision of where God is taking them in their journey of life. They need to foresee the fulfillment of their destiny and plan accordingly. Men of valor are strong and well able to handle pressure and opposition when it comes. They know they are the only ones who decide what to do with their lives and what the outcome will be.

What distinguishes a man from a boy is what you do with the challenges that come your way. Any man can run away when hard times come. Any man can blame others for what they're going through. But a mighty man rises up and faces head-on the challenges that cross his path. He rises to the occasion and are head and shoulders above those who run away. A mighty man gives his all in every arena of life. Wimps run away, warriors stay and fight. Real men stand up and face their challenges and never back down. Mighty men have the passion, the anointing, and the desire to go above and beyond the call of duty. They overcome incredible odds knowing no weapon formed against them will prosper. Mighty men have guts and determination. They don't back down when the enemy shows up. With courage they face head-on the circumstances of life.

They use and understand self-discipline. They don't let habits, desires, and short comings control them because they have developed the ability to control themselves. They have courage and self-confidence. They make good decisions and do not hesitate to carry them out. They do not doubt or waver for their confidence is nourished by actions and deeds. Men of valor do not worry or get beat down by past mistakes and they never base today's decisions based on yesterday's failures. Today is a new day and they live for the success of the present. They are quick to forgive, forget, and move forward from where they're currently at. There is no condemnation in Christ Jesus (Rom. 8:1) and they know how to forgive their own faults. They don't compare themselves today to where they were yesterday, they compare themselves to where God wants them to be. For this reason they press forward at all costs.

A real man knows that self-denial is a prerequisite to being in the Lord's army. He lives to serve his Lord and Savior, saying, "Not my will, but Your will be done." Jesus said in Luke 9:23, "If anyone desires to come after Me, let him deny himself and take up his cross daily and follow Me." In other words, you must be willing to die to yourself daily. You must lay aside your own personal will and make conscious decisions to resist those cravings and desires that are contrary to God's will. You must suppress and control all fleshly yearnings. Dying to self daily is a continual process of making right choices that align with God's will, choices that will ultimately lead to a life that reflects the character and values of Christ. Inside every warrior is a servant's heart. He is a man who dies to himself daily so that he can live for someone or something greater than himself. He lives for the complete service of another.

Woodrow Wilson said, "No man has ever risen to the true stature of spiritual manhood until he has found that it is finer to serve somebody else than it is to serve himself." A man with a servant's heart is a man others can count on. Those men others look up to the most have gained the respect of others through consistency. Whether it's doing what you say you'll do or being at the right place at the right time, being a man of valor means being consistent not once in a while but at all times. A man who is the servant of others is a man of humility. They're secure in who God made them to be that they don't need to place themselves in higher esteem than those around them. They don't seek glory and fame and are often the quickest to share the credit with those around them. Not for one second do they consider themselves more worthy or valuable.

In many cases, the church has feminized the church experience. No longer do ministers preach messages that challenge men to rise up and be the man God called them to be. Most men today have grown soft and the decay of authentic manhood is evident all around. To deliberately cultivate the virtue of toughness in a man is rarely seen on the earth today. Thankfully, 1 Cor. 16:13 tells you how to be a real man, "Be watchful, stand firm in the faith, act like men, be strong." These are all military terms. Vs. 14 then says, "Let all that you do be done in love." What God wants from you the most is that you would wake up and act like a man. He wants you to rise up every day and do what a man who loves God is supposed to do. In other words, become a man of valor. Be a mighty man, a man of integrity and honor. Don't have the mentality of Peter Pan who went around saying, "I don't want to grow up."

A mighty man denies himself totally, takes up his cross daily, and follows Christ with all his heart and soul. His life belongs to God and he gives Him permission to do with it what He pleases. Men of valor give their all in whatever endeavor they are undertaking. They pull their own weight as they strive to live up to God's holy standards of honor. Men who serve God faithfully choose to take a different path than their peers. To never become soft they choose the hard way of mental and physical and spiritual toughness. A real man craves a good fight. CEO John Neal once said, "Opposition is what we want and must have to be good at anything. Hardship is the native soil of manhood and self-reliance." A mighty man never takes the easy route. Seneca, the advisor to the emperor Nero, said, "No man is more unhappy than he who never faces adversity for he is not permitted to prove himself."

A real man does not seek after an easy life. On the contrary, they intentionally look for the kind of challenges their peers avoid and run away from. To a man of valor, this is the most fulfilling way to live, the only way to growth and progress. Their favorite verse is James 1:2, "Count it all joy when you fall into various trials." TPT says, "My fellow believers, when it seems as though you are facing nothing but difficulties, see it as an invaluable opportunity to experience the greatest joy that you can." The Phillips Bible says, "When all kinds of trials and temptations crowd into your lives, my brothers, don't resent them as intruders, but welcome them as friends." The NEB says to "count yourselves supremely happy." Men of valor are joyful in trials because they have the extreme confidence that the outcome will turn out in their favor.

In a trial all real men have a future-focused mindset. Their faith is in the God who "declares the end from the beginning" (Is. 46:10). They know when all is said and done that all will be well. Martial arts star Bruce Lee once said, "Do not pray for an easy life, pray for the strength to endure a difficult one." Don't ask for a lighter load, ask for stronger shoulders. A real man prepares for war and does not try to find an easy way out of every hardship they encounter. They just become strong in the Lord and don't care what happens. People in the world today strive for ease and comfort and because of that most modern men will follow the path of least resistance and not even try to be a real man. But men of valor are different. They fight with all they've got to be the man God wants them to be. The task is not easy but this way of life will never be more satisfying or fulfilling.

If a poster was ever made for the purpose of recruiting all males to become real men, surely these words will be on it, "The hard way is calling. Join the manhood warriors." Joining the Lord's army is voluntary and can be done by any man, in any circumstance, at any time. All that is needed is the unchanging desire to live a manly life. Men who are soft and cowardly need not apply to be in the Lord's army. God is looking for men to live by a code of manliness that is forever ready to go to war when called upon. When under attack, the world will need manly men to put on the full armor of God and do what it takes to protect and serve, to do the hard and dirty work necessary to win the war. Men of valor stay in the Word continually. They make a solid commitment to develop and maintain their fighting skills so they'll be ready when their fellow man needs them.

Men of war do not slack off in their training. They know that going to war will require the fortitude and strength that living the traditional code of manhood develops. Theodore Roosevelt said, "We need the iron qualities that go with true manhood. We need the positive virtues of resolution, of courage, of indomitable will." He also said we need the "power to do without shirking the rough work that must always be done." Be this way and you won't just be a good man, you'll be good at being a man. By striving to live the hard life you'll be armed with fire and will be forever ready to face whatever adventures and challenges that life might throw your way. Phil. 4:13 (AMP) says, "I have strength for all things in Christ who empowers me. I am ready for anything and equal to anything through Him who infuses strength into me."

Strength, courage, and honor are the primary virtues of men all over the world. They are fundamental virtues because without them no higher virtue can be attained. Warriors are not weak sissies but are "strong in the Lord and in the power of His might" (Eph. 6:10). They have the ability to dominate an opponent, to stand fast when confronted. Teddy Roosevelt lived in an age when machines and steam were taking over and a man's place in society was being questioned. Why be masculine when a machine can do the work for you? Modern men today admire Teddy Roosevelt because he and other men of his time ignored the changing culture and chose to live by the manly code even though it wasn't demanded of them. He was born into a wealthy family in New York City and could have easily settled into a life of ease and comfort. But he didn't do that. Instead, he chose what he called "the strenuous life."

By striving to live the hard way in his younger years, he armed himself with the fire and fight he needed to succeed in the challenges of his later years. All throughout his life, he had the choice to reject the masculine code but he never did. He sought to always challenge himself in the arena of life and to always carry his own weight. Teddy Roosevelt was truly a man's man. he showed that it's possible to live in our modern world of luxury and comfort and not be softened by it. He showed us that you could proactively choose to be good at being a man even when your surroundings or culture aren't conducive to exercising your inward masculinity. The world today needs more men like Teddy Roosevelt who believed that the strenuous life builds manly character. It's what makes you all that you can be.

| 11 |

"HOLY ENERGY"

In your quest to be a real man, don't go around expecting the people of the world to give you a pat on the back for all the work and effort you've put in. The world today isn't built for manhood. It's content when men act like women and women act like men. They reason why live like a man when failure to do so won't bring shame? Why live like a man when you won't be honored for it? Some say that only a sucker would try to be his best version of a man when it isn't required of him. They reason that trying to be a real man these days will simply get you taken advantage of by a culture that no longer appreciates the effort men of valor make. It is because of foolish reasonings like this that what the world needs today is a revival of men. There are way too many wimps and sissies running around.

Men need to understand that the Bible is a masculine book. Heb. 4:12 says, "For the word of God is living and powerful, and sharper than any two-edged sword." A sword divides, a sword defends, a sword defeats the enemy. Sissies don't carry swords. Jesus said, "I did not come to bring peace but a sword" (Matt. 10:34). That's masculine. Jesus is not a feminist. He's a warrior. He's the King of kings and Lord of lords. It's a masculine term when the Bible says the disciples "turned the world upside down" (Acts 17:6). The Bible talks about the sword of the Spirit and the shield of faith. Those are masculine terms. The Bible tells us to fight the good fight of faith, to endure hardness as a good soldier. The task of every man is masculine. We're told to go into all the world and preach the gospel to every creature. That's not an easy thing to do and it takes a strong man to do it.

Paul told us to "put on the whole armor of God" (Eph. 6:11). He didn't say put on your soccer shorts. It is demonic for a man to be a sissy, to be feminine, to no longer live by godly standards. Serving God is a contact sport. Be like Jesus who braided a whip and drove the money-changers out of the temple, turning over tables as He did so. We are not in a tennis match. Our fight is confrontational. This is why you need backbone to be a warrior in God's army, the confidence and mental fortitude to be ready for whatever comes. Dwight D. Eisenhower said, "There arrives that moment at which soft speaking should be abandoned and a fight to the end undertaken. Unless he is ready to fight, people will finally begin to ignore him." You are a man of God, a man of valor, and you should never be like a fine horse bred for racing that's now being used for pony rides at a party for children.

This majestic animal is tethered to a pole, he walks around in endless circles, his muscles are wasting away, and his eyes are forever downcast. Don't be that way. Rise up and show the world what it takes to be a man. You are made in the image of God and have been given the intelligence, strength, and courage to overcome all obstacles. Come alive with the ingrained masculinity inside of you. Keep the flame of your manhood burning, harness the energy and ride hard down the road of excellence. Be the type of man who exceeds the status quo. They go above and beyond what is expected of them. They're always abounding in the work of the Lord. They do not grow weary in well doing. Mighty men burn the midnight oil. Gal. 6:10 says, "As we have opportunity, let us do good to all, especially to those who are of the household of God."

Life isn't easy and, in truth, it was never meant to be. By choosing to walk on the hard path you have decided to place yourself among the most elite of all men. The main emphasis of your life is to maintain the attribute of the warrior. Doing so makes it possible for you to fulfill your God-given responsibility to provide, protect, and procreate. Sacrifice and discipline become your lifestyle for it is the only path that will allow you to leave a legacy once you are gone. Indeed, it is the only path to rich fulfillment. Is. 40:29 says God "gives power to the weak, and to those who have no might He increases strength." Go forth into battle with renewed energy and a robust spirit. You are vigorous and full of life. Within you is a readiness to act with force and enthusiasm. Nothing will stop you and continually you press forward in a powerful, forceful manner.

A man of valor always strives to do his best and remain forever ready to face the enemy in a crisis. He is always ready to rise up to the challenge before them. The truth be told, you won't become a warrior until you get sick and tired of being pushed around by the devil. There comes a time when you have to grit your teeth and fight back. It's okay to grunt! It's okay to roar! Kick yourself and prepare for war. Be the fearless warrior God created you to be. Be the type of warrior that when you pray the devil flees and heaven opens up. Become like Jesus who was the fiercest spiritual warrior the world has ever seen. Ex. 15:3 says, "The Lord is a man of war; The Lord is His name." The NIV says, "The Lord is a warrior." Rev. 19:15 says, "From His mouth comes a sharp sword so that with it He may strike the nations, and He will rule them with a rod of iron."

Yes, Jesus is a warrior and you must become just like Him. It's time to step into your calling and be the man God created you to be. It's time to wake up and prepare for war. You can't make a difference if all you do is sit on your hands and do nothing as you watch others fight the war all men have been called to fight. James 1:22 says, "But be doers of the word, and not hearers only, deceiving yourself." Martin Luther said, "The world does not need a definition of religion as much as it needs a demonstration." The Greek word for "doers" is "poietes" and is the same word used for "poet." The word carries with it the idea of creativity showing that we are all creative in some way. This word depicts someone putting forth his fullest creative abilities to achieve something. If you can't think of a manly thing to do, you must get creative.

You must put forth maximum effort and your most creative capabilities in doing what the Word tells you needs to be done in your role as a man of war. One commentator describes a doer as "a person whose life is characterized by holy energy." That energy is God's energy, a fire that is deep within you. This divine power of God is a force that empowers men and enables them to live godly lives and helps them overcome adversity. It causes them to fight with fervor. Eccl. 9:10 says, "Whatever your hand finds to do, do it with all your might." When there's fervor, there is confrontation. Warriors fight the good fight of faith. They contend earnestly for the faith (Jude 3). When there is fervor, there is continuation. They keep fighting and never back down. When there is fervor, there's consolation. One day God will say to them, "Well done, good and faithful servant."

U.S. President James Garfield got it right when he said, "I mean to make myself a man, and if I succeed in that, I shall succeed in everything else." Masculinity is simply raw energy. A man of valor wisely finds outlets to channel this masculine energy toward the collective good of those around him. God has given every warrior someone to protect, a kingdom to advance, a ministry to fulfill, a cause worth fighting for. You must wake up and prepare for war if you are to be successful in these endeavors. When opposition came against Nehemiah, he rose up and said, "Don't be afraid of them. Remember the Lord who is great and awesome" (Neh. 4:14). He then said, "Fight for your families, your sons and daughters, your wives and your homes." Men, get off the sofa, put down the video games, put away your golf clubs and fight for your family.

There's something in you that will righteously die to protect someone you love. But more than that, be willing to live to protect them physically, emotionally, and spiritually. Every woman and child, when in the presence of a man of God, shouldn't feel anything but safe. They should always feel physically, emotionally, and spiritually safe. Protect the heart of your family by having them know you'll always walk with integrity. Protect your family by giving them a sense of financial security without which there will always be tension in the home. Protect them spiritually. Pray over them and make sure they're in church every single week. They need the strength of the body of Christ to empower them to be warriors also You owe it to your family to be involved in their lives. They'll be eternally grateful for your care and support. 2 Sam. 10:12 says, "Be strong, and let us fight bravely for our people and the cities of our God."

Fight for your home! Fight for purity! Fight for victory! Fight for generosity! Fight for righteousness! You're a warrior who fights to the death! If you're not engaged in your cause, if you're not fighting for the right things, you'll instead be fighting against those things that matter most. You'll fight against authority, against your spouse, your children, and you'll fight against God. You'll fight against boredom by doing stupid things with the gifts God gave you. You'll fight against the very people who are trying to help you the most. This is what happens when you get distracted from the kingdom you're here to advance. You're called to do more than sit on the sofa, being great at golf, having a nice house and car. You were created to advance the kingdom of God so don't get distracted.

The problem is a distracted warrior is always a destructive warrior. This is why you must never abandon your post. Do not walk away from your calling. Do not surrender that which you were called to do. Your ministry is to advance the kingdom of God on the earth. This is your contribution to the world. Matt. 6:33 says to "seek ye first the advancement of the kingdom of God and His righteousness." Jesus calls you "the light of the world" so let your light shine every single day. You're an ambassador of heaven. You're sent by God from heaven to the earth to represent the love of God. You are a mighty man of valor. You're brave, you're confident, you're unwavering. You always fight for what is right. You're here to conquer and take ground for the kingdom. You're here to win. God created you with the heart of a warrior and you were born and bred to fight the good fight. Prepare for war for you may be the only example of a godly warrior that some people will ever see.

David said in Ps. 144:1, "Blessed be the Lord my Rock, who trains my hands for war, and my fingers for battle." The heart of a warrior is inside of you so stop being so passive! Get in the battle! Wake up and prepare for war! Is the devil attacking you? Then do something about it! Declare war! Take him down! Be free from the burdens that hinder you. Be like Jesus and turn over some tables as you take a whip and chase the devil out of your life. God trains you to be ready for battle. Manhood is not a playground, it's a battleground. Author Robert Jordan said, "There is one rule above all others for being a man. Whatever comes, face it on your feet." Grit your teeth and run to the roar for there is a battle to be fought. People, whether they admit it or not, want to know they can depend on men when things get hard. They cringe at a man who falls to pieces in the face of adversity.

The world is looking for their fathers and husbands to stand strong and be able to take action. When chaos explodes, its almost invariably left to the men to handle the situation. Fighting and violence are at the very core of masculinity. It's this amazing power and energy that drove the Vikings and the Spartans to gain mastery over their enemies. In the movie "Fight Club" a question is asked, "How much can you know about yourself if you've never been in a fight?" How can you know if you'll get back up if you've never been knocked down? The ancients of old understood that moral courage and physical courage were of the same essence. Building up a man's strength in the boxing ring would help him be a better all-around man. Philosopher Lucius Seneca said, "Without an adversary, strength shrivels. We see how great and valuable strength is when, by endurance, it shows what it is capable of."

There has never been a better time to be alive. God's plan since before time began is about to unfold all over the world and He wants you to be a part of it. Jesus said in Matt. 11:12, "From the days of John the Baptist until now the kingdom of God is advancing forcefully, and forceful men lay hold of it." We battle not against flesh and blood but against powers and principalities of this dark world. There's a fight inside of you. Release it! Let it come to life! Don't sit back but engage in the battle. Pick up your sword and slay that dragon who is terrorizing your life. Step into your mission. Step into your calling. Fulfill your destiny. Wake up and prepare for war. You are a man of God.

You are a warrior. Greater is He who is in you than he who is in the world. If you're in Christ, you have the same Spirit that raised Jesus from the dead dwelling in you.

God is going to establish His rule and cover the earth with His glory by pouring Himself into those men who throw off the cloak of passivity and put on the whole armor of God. We live in a world at war and we're supposed to fight back. Anyone who chooses to become a Christian automatically enters God's military and is immediately engaged in the longest war ever fought. Life is a battle, a struggle, and there is no such thing as an easy life. To win the battle you must rise above your circumstances and be the victor instead of the victim. There is a real divine power that can be resident in your life that helps you overcome whatever obstacles you face in life. God in you will make you stronger than whatever trial you are facing. You have greater capacity than you think. There is truly a God who lives inside of you, a godly Spirit that makes you stronger in the heat of battle.

You have a strength that gives you peace, stability, and assurance because Jesus has already conquered the world and He lives inside of you. You are strong because God has made you strong. When darkness pushes against you, step in and fight back. Sometimes you turn a cheek, other times you turn over a table. You are a warrior and you are called to win major battles in life. Those who are fearful and weak don't take risks. They choose comfort and security over opportunity. A warrior reflects courageous energy and is characterized by initiative, protection, provision, and perseverance. A warrior is a man of action, a person who tackles life head-on and wins. He takes the other guy's best shot and still stands strong and continues to move forward. He looks fear in the eye and spits in its face. He does not allow fear to handicap his ability to fight and move forward.

A warrior works the hardest and the longest and outlasts the competition. He perseveres in the midst of all kinds of adversity and fights for what matters most. He takes the initiative and does not run away from problems and is most comfortable on the battlefield. He has an inner supply of conquering energy and with holy boldness makes an impact on the world. A warrior is assertive but gets his direction from God. This is not about power, it's about strength of character. It's not a destructive force, it's a positive energy force. A warrior fights with purpose for noble things and eternal values. He has a reason to fight and is constructive and intentional. He runs the race to win staying alert and in top condition at all times. Warriors are those who "mount up with wings like eagles. They shall run and not be weary, they shall run and not faint" (Is. 40:31). They fight the good fight of faith and never back down.

| 12 |

"LEAP OF FAITH"

In every time and place throughout all of human history, courage was an essential condition, a thing that was absolutely necessary if you wanted to be called a man. All the great dynasties of times past all had one thing in common, and that was to equate courage with manliness. A real man develops courage and is ready to take risks. For courage to exist, there must be a risk. In order to grow strong and develop into a real man, a man of valor, there must be a little danger in your life. Manhood is an earned status, an achievement. Just as it can be earned, it can also be lost. Thus, a man who doesn't risk having his manhood taken away, is not a man at all. Our enemy the devil prowls around like a roaring lion seeking whom he may devour (1 Peter 5:8). This being so, opportunities to exercise manly courage through taking risks are plentiful.

To make risk-taking rewarding, you need to, as psychologist Nicholas Hobbs puts it, "Choose trouble for oneself in the direction of what one would like to become." In most cultures, risk-taking was encouraged in young men as a way for them to gain the strength and boldness to tackle the hard and mature tasks of later life. The bottom line is that there is no manliness without risk. To take a risk gives a man the chance to prove he can thrive in times of hardship and uncertainty. A real man will engage in risky behavior. The stakes are terrifying yet thrilling. When taking a risk one wrong move could mean death but success brings honor, respect, and masculinity. Make no mistake about it, the path to manhood runs through risk. Taking a healthy, positive risk is one of those things that can make you feel fully like a man.

Psychologist Roy Baumeister said, "A woman is entitled to respect until she loses it. A man must earn respect. He must repeatedly achieve, obtain, surpass, conquer." What is a risk? It's any decision or behavior that comes with a significant probability of a negative outcome. Let's face it, almost all decisions come with a risk. Develop risk-taking tendencies. When there is something you really want, recognize that you have to push yourself more than the average guy and take risks they're not willing to take. Start small and work your way up. As you take smaller risks and experience success, you'll gain the confidence and motivation that you can use to take bigger risks. Step into the arena of life and prove yourself a man by taking a risk. Yes, you may sometimes fail but you'll be a better man because you put forth the effort.

In the ancient code of manhood there is no dishonor in striving and falling short. Author David Gilmore said, "The worst sin of manliness is not honest failure but cowardly withdrawal." The truth be told, taking risks is the fuel for greatness.

Nobody ever became great without a lifestyle of taking risks over and over again. Real men need risks in order to survive. Masculinity is not something that is given to you but something you gain. You gain it by taking risks and by winning both small and big battles with honor. John Eldredge said men are "wild at heart" and there is no better way of going on an adventure to discover this wildness than to take a risk. With great risk comes great reward. Poet T. S. Eliot said, "Only those who will risk going too far can possibly find out how far one can go."

Be bold. Step into the unknown and take a leap of faith. Trust God and attempt an endeavor that the world says has little chance of success. With a leap of faith Noah obeyed God and built an ark to save his family from the flood. Also, by faith Abraham prepared to sacrifice his son believing God would provide a lamb. Consider David who by faith took a risk and confronted a giant with only a sling and a stone. Consider Peter who stepped out of the boat when Jesus invited him to come. Exercising faith in God often requires taking a risk. 2 Cor. 5:7 says, "For we walk by faith, not by sight." A biblical step of faith is backed up by assurance and certainty. A leap of faith is not a blind leap or an irrational impulse that causes you to jump out into the great unknown without prayer or any forethought.

Taking risks for the sake of God's work and kingdom is a sign of faith and obedience. Blind, reckless risks, however, are discouraged because a leap of faith requires wisdom and discretion. Men of valor who take risks and leaps of faith do so because they trust in God who they know is powerful enough to hold them up and not let them fall (Jude 24). Taking a risk means you'll have to leave the safety of your comfort zone. Peter abandoned his safety and comfort when he jumped out of the boat to walk on water to Jesus. When you demonstrate an authentic trust in God, you will quickly find out that a leap of faith is actually a leap into His all-powerful and loving arms. He delights when you have the boldness to take a risk because your actions show that you trust Him completely. He delights in your trust and will reward you because of it.

Risks taken in faith, trusting in God's guidance and provision, is commendable. He always responds to faith that manifests itself in taking risks and stepping out by trusting Him. Taking risks without prayer, seeking counsel, or considering potential consequences, is not considered godly risk-taking. Risks taken foolishly are always condemned. At the same time, if your risk-taking is in faith with complete trust in God, it cannot be foolish no matter how incredible the risk or unlikely the outcome. Risk isn't comfortable but, when motivated by faith, it is the right thing to do. Esther risked her life to save her people from annihilation by going to her husband the king unannounced. The Bible portrays taking risks as a way to demonstrate faith in God's power and promises. Esther knew it's better to risk your life than to waste it.

Risk-taking helps build your trust in God. Even as you face the unknown, even when you can't see the outcome, take the risk because God is surely with you. God wants you to take risks. If you play it safe all the time then you won't need any faith and the Bible says that without faith it is impossible to please God (Heb. 11:6). In the parable of the talents God condemned the servant who buried his talent in the ground. He took no risks and was called "a wicked and lazy servant" (Matt. 25:26). Faith is not something you know and believe, it's something you do. You can't have faith without taking some kind of risk. Risk-taking is the evidence that you have faith. When you take risks in faith, God will steer you toward a life that He will eventually use mightily. He will always be faithful to you, protecting you all the way.

You're really not living unless you're taking risks. Acts 15:26 says Paul and Barnabas were "men who risked their lives for the name of our Lord Jesus Christ." In today's world, risk-takers are needed more than ever because men are being marginalized. They're treated as if they're insignificant and society is pushing them to the point of being powerless. Men are belittled and it's almost politically incorrect to say you're proud to be a man, or that men should act like men. This is why the greatest need in the world today are men who are risk-takers. The world needs men who will rise up and become what God created them to be. They need men who will not be bought or sold, men who in their innermost souls are true and honest. They need men who do not fear to call sin by its name, men whose conscious is clear and pure. In a world that is morally unraveling, God is looking for men who will stand up for what's right though the heavens fall.

God did not save you to be an average, normal man. You're not called to do what unsaved people do. You're not called to be a pew-sitter Sunday after Sunday. You're called to make a positive impact wherever you go. To do that, you must accept what God said about you. Rom. 8:37 says, "Yet in all these things we are more than conquerors through Him who loved us." Celebrate that God made you the way you are. Celebrate that He made you a mighty man. When the devil says you can't withstand the storm, you tell him, "I am the storm!" You are a warrior and you always show the devil who's boss. You are stronger than all the things he throws at you. You are stronger than your past, stronger than all the challenges coming in your future. Warriors don't look for trouble but they don't back down from it either. Mighty men are unstoppable because they have courage and integrity of character. The term "mighty men" is used 71 times in the Bible.

If you don't believe you are a mighty man, you will always be mentally defeated and emotionally wounded. You will conduct your life on the lowest levels of society, never rising above life's challenges. Never! God wants you to live an extraordinary life, a life lived radically and explored intentionally. He wants you to stand out in a mediocre world instead of always fitting in. God wants you to have a spiritual awakening to see who you really are. You are more than a conqueror! You are a warrior! Burning in the heart of every warrior is desire, drive, determination, and fire. Warriors do not back down. They do not relent. Warriors say, "Trouble, here I come!' Respect is not given, it is earned. Warriors tell their enemies, "Come at me! I dare you! It's time for war!" A warrior is always ready for battle. Sleeping in is for grandmas. Warriors are up at the crack of dawn and are ready for war. Warriors don't quit! They don't back down!

They show up for battle in rain, hail, or sunshine. Warriors don't back down from pain; they face their pain. They push back harder and tell pain, "Give me more!" Push through the pain and you'll be a stronger you. You'll have a stronger body, a stronger mind, and a stronger character. You'll rise up and give more than what's asked of you. Quitting is for those who have no heart. Loses quit. Wimps quit. Sissies quit. Warriors do not quit! They fight on against all odds. They keep going. Men are unstoppable when they have strength, courage, and integrity of character. You are the hero of those you care about. Therefore, you have to develop a warrior mindset. God breathed His life into you and made you a mighty man of valor. Jesus is a warrior and 2 Cor. 3:18 says you "are being transformed into the same image from glory to glory."

You are who God says you are. If He says you are a mighty man of valor, then believe it and start acting like it. The Bible says, "Greater is He who is in you than he who is in the world" (1 John 4:4). Believing that will cause you to never lack integrity and courage. Andrew Jackson once said, "One man with courage is a majority." Rom. 8:31 says, "If God be for us, who can be against us?" Josh. 1:6 says, "Be strong and of good courage." Notice the two-letter word "be." When God tells you to be something, there is created power in that word. For example, when God brought the world into existence, He said, "Let there be light" (Gen. 1:3), and there was light. Jesus told the leper "be clean" (Matt. 8:3) and immediately his leprosy was cleansed. When God tells you to be strong, His power will be there to make you strong. God will never tell you to be something you cannot be. Be encouraged by that. Say out loud, "I am strong."

If He tells you to be strong, you can be strong. If He tells you to have good courage, you can have good courage. It takes divine strength to be the man God created you to be. To have courage in today's world, you've got to be strong. What is courage? It's the state of mind that enables you to face danger with confidence, resolution, and bravery. Life shrinks or expands in proportion to your courage to be who God says you are. Men who are trying to reinvent themselves don't know who God said they already are. Go to your secret place, close your eyes, shut your mouth. and listen to what the still, small voice of God is telling you. All sissies do is talk. They never listen nor do they put in the effort to be great. Sissies talk; warriors listen. James 1:19, "Let every man be swift to hear and slow to speak." What you hear God say will bring you the quality of life that you need to be a mighty man of God.

You're to live your life by faith in who God said you are. He said you're a mighty man of valor so act like it. Warriors do not have a spirit of fear but of power, love and a sound mind (2 Tim. 1:7). This is what makes them more than a conqueror. Courage enlarges itself through adversity. Every David needs a Goliath, and every Daniel needs a den of lions. There is no victory without confrontation and war. This is why you're told to fight the good fight of faith. Your stripes aren't earned having a Sunday picnic, they're earned on the battlefield. Who you are and what you become is all based on how you handle the adversity that comes into your life. The same boiling water that makes a potato soft will make an egg hard. Adversity don't change men; it exposes them for who they really are. All men will face challenges. They will be tested to see if they truly are a man.

Understand that challenges come because of the warrior inside you. But know this, you can't be a coward and a traitor and expect God to give you the best He has to offer. It's the testing of your faith that produces in you a warrior spirit. All men become warriors when they face and defeat challenges that are bigger than are. The successful warrior is the man with laser-like focus, the man who keeps his eyes on Jesus. Focus is a power. Whatever you focus on will get better and stronger. David said, "I will fear no evil; For You are with me" (Ps. 23:4). He had laser-like focus and was able to go out and defeat the giant who stood before him. Warriors trust God, wimps and sissies don't. Standing strong against your enemies is an act of faith and obedience, running away is an act of unbelief and disobedience.

Prepare for war knowing every victorious warrior draws his strength from the Lord above. That's where his focus is. Victorious warriors win first, and then they go to war. Warriors exist in a universe of possibilities. They follow their dreams with passion and certainty. The warrior knows better days are ahead if they'll fight with all their heart. Warriors have the heart of a lion. They do not back down. They do not relent. They are bold and have courage and unwavering faith. They are not survivors. They don't survive; they thrive! Prov. 30:30 tells of the strength and fearlessness of a lion when it says, "A lion, which is mighty among beasts, and does not turn away from any." Warriors are built from the struggle, formed from pain, strengthened by adversity. They have the ability to face difficulties and challenges with strength and determination.

Warriors make the best of bad situations. They see the opportunity in the struggle. They fight with confidence because they have a strong and unwavering faith in God's power and protection. Their courage is a reflection of their trust in God's promises and providence. They grow strong in trial and hardship. Going through the worst of times ensures their story will be a great one. Their bravery is found not in themselves but in the steadfast love and faithfulness of God. Adversity turns them from being a zero to a hero, from nothing to something, from the bottom to the top. They embrace courage in times of trial and uncertainty. Instead of succumbing to fear, they choose to stand firm with the knowledge that God is always with them. Warriors are always prepared for battle, prepared to soar above all trial and conflict. Embrace your challenges. Have the heart of a lion and push through them like the warrior you are.

| 13 |

"WORTH FIGHTING FOR"

The will of God is not for you to just be a good man, but to be good at being a man. Manliness, then, can be described as living a life of excellence and virtue. What is godly virtue? It's a firm and habitual disposition to do good at all times. It allows the man of valor to not only perform good deeds but to give the best of himself. Virtue is the crown that a warrior wears upon his head. It adds beauty, grace, and refinement to his life. It takes his masculine energy and channels it toward worthy ends. The virtue of a warrior refers to oral excellence and good character that is a reflection of God's character and is pursued through a life of faith, hope, and love. These three theological virtues are fundamental to a man's life of virtue. Faith is believing in God, hope is trusting in God's promises, and love is acting with compassion and kindness toward others.

Prudence and wisdom, justice and fairness, fortitude and courage, and temperance and self-control are also considered essential for a life of virtue. At the same time, Aristotle said that courage is the mother of all virtues. For sure, in a world that is not virtuous, it is a brave thing to go out there and do what needs to be done. Godly virtue is about consistently displaying high moral standards and acting in a way that aligns with God's will. It chooses to do what is right and strives for spiritual growth. 1 Tim. 4:16 (TPT) says, "Give careful attention to your spiritual life and every cherished truth you teach, for living what you preach will release salvation inside you." A man's claim to virtue is weak if he doesn't have the courage and strength to back it up when challenged. He needs the fire of the Holy Spirit and a willingness to fight when necessary.

Theodore Roosevelt said, "You will not be able to hold your own in the outside world if you do not have manliness and courage on the inside of you." He went on to say, "It does no good to have either of these two sets of qualities if you lack the other." He is saying a man of virtue must be brave as well as gentle and tender. He said his father was a man who "combined the strength and courage and will and energy of the strongest man with the tenderness, cleanness, and purity of a woman." A virtuous man is a godly man whose life is characterized by a deep commitment to living a life pleasing to God. He models his life after the example of Jesus. He shows compassion and kindness to others, walks in honesty and uprightness, is forever loyal to his Lord and Savior, and acknowledges God's role in all aspects of life.

English poet Benjamin Johnson said, "When a virtuous man is raised, it brings gladness to his friends, grief to his enemies, and glory to his posterity." A virtuous man knows he wasn't created for comfort but for greatness. He knows he was created and chosen by God to help make the lives of other people better. All men should strive for virtue and excellence every day of their lives. C. S. Lewis wrote, "Something deep in the human heart breaks at the thought of a life of mediocrity." A real man is not content to sit down and drift along with the world around him. Men at their best have something unique to offer the world no matter what the culture says. To be a man of moral excellence you must dig deep inside yourself. In your inner man the elements of masculinity are sitting like a well-trained army that is ready to fight at any time.

The spirit of masculinity is like a power switch on the inside of you that is waiting to be turned on. When you flip the switch the warrior inside of you gets activated. You are wild at heart, and it is your responsibility to prepare for war, to release the warrior inside of you, the spiritual, primal part that is deeply ingrained in a man's soul. Turn on the power inside of you and flip on the motivation that allows you to reach your full potential, to be all that God gloriously created you to be. When this power is turned on, you'll feel alive, invigorated, motivated to be your best, and just plain manly. You'll run toward the giant in front of you and not away from him. Standing in front of David when he faced Goliath was an opportunity to reveal his toughness, his resiliency, his manhood. It was a challenge he would not back away from.

There are four types of men in the world: warriors, winners, whiners, and wimps. The world celebrates warriors, enjoy winners, get frustrated with whiners, and have disgust for the wimp. What each of these four types of men have in common is each of them has earned the title they bear. They earned their title based on how they responded to struggle and adversity. Make no mistake about it, there is no shortage of struggle in this life, both great and small. Job 5:7 says, "Yet man is born to trouble, as the sparks fly upward." How will you know the valor and courage of a warrior unless you endure the adversity of battle? How can we crown a champion unless we've seen them struggle and overcome to be a winner? How will we know who the whiner is unless trouble breaks out and all they do is complain? How do we know who the wimp is until we see them ignore a problem hoping somebody else will solve it?

Real men are motivated to take on large challenges that will give them the opportunity to gain God's approval, to prove themselves as men of high status in the Lord's army. Pleasing God is what propels and pushes men to not back down from a challenge and motivates them to accomplish big things and strive for greatness. Sad to say, when men opt out of manning up and decide to live a life of safety, society around them dissolves into a state of moral and cultural decline. The question to be asked is, "How will you respond when a trial comes your way?" Will you engage like the warrior, complain like the whiner, ignore it like the wimp, or be the winner God created you to be? Men earn their titles by how they respond when a crisis comes their way. For example, the Angel of the Lord appeared to Gideon and said, "The Lord is with you, you mighty man of valor" (Judges 6:12).

How did Gideon respond to this wonderful proclamation? He asked, "If the Lord is with us, why then has all this happened to us?" (vs. 13). He was whining before the Lord. In Judges 4, the prophetess Deborah commanded Barak to go to war against their enemies. Barak said to her, "If you will go with me, then I will go; but if you do not go with me, I will not go" (vs. 8). Barak was being a wimp here. He refused to go into battle unless a woman went with him. You cannot change what you will not confront. Ignoring the problem doesn't make it go away. Stop whining about what you wish would change and stop ignoring what you're too afraid to change. Whiners and wimps do nothing and remain losers all their lives. Make up your mind to be a warrior. Man up knowing that in Christ the blood of greatness is in your veins. Confess out loud, "Greater is He who is in me than he who is in the world" (1 John 4:4).

Declare boldly, "The strength of the Holy One inside me surpasses all the world's opposition." You have to make up your mind to be a warrior. It's a choice you make. Decide to be a warrior and bring about change in the world you live in. What do warriors do? Through faith they subdue kingdoms, work righteousness, obtain promises, stop the mouths of lions (Heb. 11:33). In simple terms, they overcome. There is always victory in Jesus. The word "overcome" is the Greek word "nikao" and it means 'to conquer, to be victorious or to prevail in the face of obstacles.' Webster's Dictionary says "overcome" means 'to vanquish, to subdue, to surmount, to get the better of, to overcome difficulties, to gain the superiority.'

Men of valor reject passivity. They are brave and strong with unflinching courage. They're not timid like some children, not faint-hearted like some women, not cowardly like some men. To overcome is the state of being more than a conqueror, to be in a settled state of victory. John uses the word seven times in Revelation to describe believers and the blessings they receive. Warriors know that the forces of evil are fighting a losing battle. Jesus won the victory over evil on the cross and that victory belongs to every warrior in the Lord's army. John MacArthur said, "True believers have nothing to fear, for even Satan's hosts with their perversions can't take them out of the Lord's hands." This should give all men great confidence. David Guzik said, "The believer has a resource for victory, the vital presence of the indwelling Jesus which makes victory always possible."

Unfortunately, not every man has tapped into his inner need for risk and adventure and decided not to meet the challenge to be great. Most men today still choose to play it safe. They run away from trouble. They keep silent when they should speak up. They get passive when they should be combative. It is through trial and chaos that men become great. Men of valor are those who when given the chance to rise to the occasion admirably answer the call to do so. No soldier in the army of the Lord can be timid and passive on the battlefield. They do things that allow them to stand apart from other men. Indeed, they must be bold and aggressive. Warriors are never concerned about how many enemy forces are coming against them. Mighty men never avoid confrontation. They don't say, "How many are they?" They say, "Where are they?"

Warriors don't need an alarm clock. Their goals, their desires, and their purpose wakes them up each and every day. Warriors are not ordinary. There is nothing average about them. Warriors are resilient, they endure, they dig deep within themselves. There is nothing they cannot be, do, or have. A warrior never compares himself with others. The only competition for a warrior is the man in the mirror. Warriors know that their choices create their reality and their responses create their outcome. Warriors will fight for a better future. They will fight to leave a legacy. They stay true to the vision inside of them. Warriors want more and will be more because they will give more. They will give more effort, more pain, more sacrifice, more heart, more courage. The pain they feel today will be replaced with the strength they'll need tomorrow. Be a warrior! Live your dreams! Be fearless! Pain is temporary but greatness lasts forever.

God created all men with a warrior spirit, a warrior attitude. Men of valor strive for greatness. Yes, sometimes you will fall but the true warrior gets back up and keeps pressing forward. The real virtue is found in the striving. Whatever blood, sweat, and tears you pour out will be returned to you in the form of greater strength and deeper satisfaction. You can try to float through life by seeking comfort and avoiding challenge but if you do that you'll end up being weak and a soft shell of a man. God did not make you to be soft like a marshmallow. He made you to be strong and vigorous. Rise up and never let your drive for greatness be denied and left unsatisfied. You were created with limitless potential, capabilities, and possibilities. There is no mountain so high that you can't climb it and no ocean so wide that you can't swim it.

The Lord is a warrior (Ex. 15:3) and you've been made in His image. You have been given all the strength God can possibly give a man without making them God. Good things happen when men rise up and become the warrior God created them to be. If there is a warrior in the home, there is nothing the family will have to worry about. This means there is nothing you can't conquer. All you have to do is wake up and prepare for war. God is looking for men of dignity and integrity, men who are warriors who will fight and protect. In God's search for mighty men, will He find you? Will you flip on the power switch of masculinity that is inside of you? Will you rise up from the bed of slumber and strive for greatness? By all means, push yourself to be great. A man at his peak uses all of his potential and becomes all he is capable of becoming. In other words, what a man can be, he must be.

It is heartbreaking that all over the world women are involved in church activities and the things of God more than men. Why is this? The church has softened and feminized manhood. Men are treated like they're women and this is wrong. In too many homes the wives are telling the husbands what to do. Worse yet, the men are letting them do it. The church has created transvestites out of their men. They want men to act like women, to be wimpy instead of the warrior they really are. No where in scripture is a mighty man of God a wimp. He's much, much more than a soft-bellied nice guy. God created in men the desire to fight for what is right. Great things happen when men fight for the right cause. Before David faced Goliath he said to his older brother who ridiculed him, "Is there not a cause?" (1 Sam. 17:29). Real men fight for a cause.

They find things worth fighting for and then go to war for that cause.

Is not advancing the kingdom of God on the earth a worthy cause to fight for? Having a good marriage, raising godly children, and fulfilling your destiny are all causes worth fighting for. God uses men to do a great work on the earth. Not just any man, but mighty men, men who will face their enemies and not back down. God needs men who are ready and willing to do a mighty work on the earth. A mighty man is a real man with real responsibilities with real focus and real intent to do the right things that bring glory to God. They are mature men who are willing to lay down their life for the cause they are fighting for. Something powerful happens inside of a man when he finds a cause for which to fight. A rush of adrenaline flows through him as he night and day focuses on his cause. He believes he is unstoppable, that he can do anything. There is no stopping a man with a cause. What he does will echo through eternity. He will leave a legacy that will be known for generations.

God made us to be fighting warriors. Mighty men are made to fight for a cause. Until a man finds a cause for which he is willing to fight and die, he never truly lives. Without a cause to fight for, men get internally bored and that's when bad things happen. A man without a cause will begin to rebel against authority and will self-destruct. This is what happened to David. He stayed home when he should have gone to war with his men. He lost his cause and ended up sleeping with Bathsheba. This one act destroyed the rest of his life. Warriors are certain about the direction they're going in life. They know what their cause is. If David would have stayed true to his cause, none of these bad things would have happened. Warriors are certain about the direction they're going in life. They know what their cause is. It's time to be a warrior! It's time to fight for your cause! You have more potential than you can possibly imagine.

You are capable of doing anything. God has given you so much strength that when used correctly you will be unstoppable. There is zero hesitation in the warrior. He says, "I can! I will! I must!" It's all in or not in at all. He will not back down! He will not yield! He will fight until his last breath and do everything to win! The warrior says, "I've got this! I am ready! I will act now! I will fight with everything inside of me!" The warrior will fight for what is right no matter the odds. The warrior says, "I am more than a conqueror! I will not be defeated! It's not over until I say it's over." You are a warrior! Warriors never back down and they never quit! They run toward the giants in their life knowing no weapon wormed against them will prosper (Is. 54:17). Pick up your sword and fight for what you believe in. Stand tall in your confidence. Be strong in your faith. Stand up and shout the war cry. AAR-RGGHH!!!

| 14 |

"HOLY CALLING"

The life you've been given will include moments that involve taking a risk and stepping into the unknown. This is why you need to learn the way of the warrior. The truth be told, striving for an easy life is not a realistic goal to have. Jesus said in Matt. 10:34 (MSG), "Don't think I've come to make life cozy." It should come as no surprise to you that being a warrior is a central theme of the entire Bible. The Old Testament tells stories of a warrior God and a warrior people. All throughout history men have strived to be a lean, mean, fighting machine. From birth the Spartans nurtured and trained their boys to grow up and become mighty warriors. Japan had their valiant, fearless, and lionhearted samurai warriors whose undaunted courage came from living life as if they were already dead.

Deep reverence is given to men like William Wallace and General Maximus who embodied what it means to be a warrior, to be a man who fights for what he believes in. Unfortunately, today's world is fighting against men having the warrior mentality. Men today are taught to avoid confrontation and to get in touch with their feminine side. The result of this wayward thinking is the creation of the ultimate Mr. Nice Guy. These are the men who avoid conflict and aggression even when it is called for and justified. Society pushes men to be sweet and sensitive not realizing that properly tapping into the warrior's energy provides a man with unsurpassable power to fulfill his destiny. A warrior's energy is needed not only in times of war but on all the battlefields of life. It helps him reach his goals, fight for worthy causes, to achieve greatness.

Giants will surely come your way and you must be a mighty warrior to defeat them. John 10:10 says, "The thief comes to steal, kill, and destroy." Therefore, becoming an aggressive warrior is not optional, it's essential. A warrior needs to be aggressive as he faces the forces of the enemy head on. He is always competitive and continually makes an all-out effort to win and succeed. Men of valor harness their aggression and use it as a mighty force that pushes him to be the best he can be and to move him forward toward his goals. Warriors know why they're here. They have a clear and definite purpose in life. Those who don't feel lost and restless for he is drifting along instead of marching forward. Men of valor are always alert and forever vigilant. They have keen situational awareness. They are always watching, observing, studying, and planning.

A real man's courage is rooted in the fact that he is not afraid to die. The brevity of life brings clarity to his mind thus he makes every day and every decision count. He is decisive and not afraid to make bold decisions. He is cool, calm, and collected when under pressure. Once a decision is made, he moves on it because he does not live in regret. He trains himself and is prepared for moments when important decisions have to be made. He's thinking before the crisis arrives and when it does come, he instinctively knows what to do. All warriors in the Lord's army are highly disciplined. His power is rooted in self-control. He is the master of his energies, releasing them and pulling back as he chooses. His discipline frees him from the fear of pain. He believes pain is just weakness leaving the body. He relishes hard times and difficulty because it makes him stronger.

Warriors always sees things from God's perspective even if no one else does. David saw Goliath as a defeated foe when everyone else feared for their safety. He saw the outcome of this battle because God was the source of his strength and protection. He said in Ps. 28:7, "The Lord is my strength and my shield; My heart trusted in Him, and I am helped." Warriors know that God is sovereign and in control over all things. Ps. 22:28 says, "For dominion belongs to the Lord, and He rules over the nations." This verse illustrates God's ultimate authority and influence as does Col. 1:17 where Paul said, "He is before all things, and in Him all things hold together." Warriors overcome challenges and adversity by relying on a higher power. They run to God for strength during difficult times viewing Him as a source of support and resilience.

David said in 1 Sam. 17:45, "You come to me with sword, spear, and javelin, but I come to you in the name of the Lord of hosts, the God of the armies of Israel, whom you have defied." Vs. 47, "And everyone assembled here will know that the Lord rescues His people, but not with sword and spear. This is the Lord's battle, and He will give you to us." In David's eyes, it was God who was fighting Goliath and not himself. The giant was bigger and more powerful than David, but he certainly was no match for the God of David. David knew this and boldly stepped out with the confidence that comes from God. His faith and assurance were not in his own ability, but the fact that God was with him. There comes a time when you have to step out and put action to what you believe in. Real faith will compel you to act, to run toward the giant who mockingly stands before you.

In the kingdom of God there is no place for those who wish to have nothing to do in the war against good and evil. You are either a warrior for God or a godless pagan. The day you gave your life to Christ was the day you were summoned to active duty in the Lord's army. Paul says that God "saved us and called us to a holy calling" (2 Tim. 1:9). Jesus warned that we would face difficulties in life and urged His followers to be ready for them (John 16:1-4). He knew that those not trained for battle will ultimately be defeated. Life is a battleground and without the way of the warrior the enemy will surely get a stronghold on your life. This is why warriors must be trained to face the dangers and struggles of daily living. Warriors are trained in the boot camp of life. All their life they're taught how to engage in combat or warfare with the ultimate goal of survival and victory.

To train means to develop or form habits, thoughts, and behavior by discipline. It means to make proficient by instruction and lots and lots of practice. David said in Ps. 18:34, "He teaches my hands to make war, so that my arms can bend a bow of bronze." Vs. 39, "For You have armed me with strength for the battle." A successful warrior is one who is prepared. They train over and over and over again. They train because when the real battle takes place, they'll know what to do. They'll respond by instinct because that is what they were trained to do. Heroic actions are the by-product of instinct; of the training you have gone through. Instinct and training is developed in the unseen preparation of a warrior. David was able to kill Goliath because of the training he went through with the lion and the bear.

Warriors must commit to training, to doing the right thing over and over again until it becomes a habit. A thought determines an action, an action determines a habit, a habit determines your future. 1 Tim. 4:7 (AMP) says, "Train yourself toward godliness, keeping yourself spiritually fit." The NLT says, "Spend your time and energy in training yourself for spiritual fitness." Training takes great discipline and a determined investment of all your energies. Indeed, the way of the warrior is a stripped-down, disciplined, sweaty affair. High-spirited spiritual training and discipline is essential to your preparation with the understanding that discipline is necessary to accomplish anything of value in this life. Discipline is a picture of vigorous, persevering, and strenuous self-sacrifice that a warrior goes through in order to win the battle he is engaged in.

Heb. 12:11 (TPT), "Now all discipline seems to be painful at the time, yet later it will produce a transformation of character." It is the well-trained that find themselves ready for battle. Spiritual training enables you to do the job you've been called to do. It equips you for works of service, to do the same works Jesus did when He walked the earth (John 14:12). You will unlikely be able to imitate the works of Jesus without imitating His lifestyle, and this is where spiritual training comes in. To walk like Jesus, you must walk with Jesus. You must spend quality time with the Father like Jesus did (Matt. 14:23). Spiritual training revolves around spiritual disciplines such as prayer and a continual study of the scriptures. Study the life of Jesus and see His attitude and actions. See how He disciplined Himself and showed love and mercy to others. Do what He did and you'll be ready for combat at a moment's notice.

Warriors train to learn what it is they need to do, but knowing the right way isn't always the same as doing it. You've got to live it out, and that takes practice. Paul said in Phil. 4:9 (TPT), "Now put into practice everything you have heard, observed, and learned from me, and the God of peace will be with you." The Greek word for "practice" is "prasso" and it refers to repetition or continuous action. You develop the ability to do the right thing by doing the right thing. 1 John 3:7 says, "Let no one deceive you, whoever practices righteousness is righteous." If you aren't practicing what you know to be right, you won't go anywhere in life. Paul told Timothy, "Practice these things, immerse yourself in them, so that all may see your progress" (1 Tim. 4:15). Training must always be followed by practice.

Warriors train until they can do what needs to be done by instinct. Warriors don't go to the gym to train once; they go day after day after day. They train continually so they'll know what to do when the battle comes their way. Warriors wake up and prepare for war! How do they do that? Training! Practice! Training! Practice! That's what mighty warriors do. That's how and why they win the fight. They prepare for war! They meditate on the promises of God over and over again. They pray without ceasing. They do these things over and over again for this is what builds strength in their faith and inner man. What they do over and over is what determines how they'll respond in the middle of the battle Training takes time. No champion athlete got there by doing one push-up. They trained hard for years. What are you doing over and over again? Whatever it is will be revealed when the fighting starts.

Spiritual conflict is intended to establish dominance over the opposition. Fighting involves intense effort for it is a struggle that requires maximum exertion. David said in Ps. 144:1, "Blessed be the Lord my Rock, who trains my hands for war, and my fingers for battle." You train because there are wars to fight, battles to win, and a race to run. Heb. 12:1 (AMP) says, "Let us run with patient endurance and steady and active persistence the appointed course of the race that is set before us." The Greek word translated "race" is "agon" from which we get the English word "agony." The word means 'a contest, battle, conflict, fight.' This race you're running is not a casual Sunday afternoon jog. The reality is it's a difficult and often agonizing war and it will take training and practice to come out victorious.

In order to win warriors are also trained to follow instructions at all times. David said in Ps. 5:8 (MSG), "And here I am waiting for directions to get me safely through enemy lines." David asked for instructions from God before going into battle. He asked God in 1 Chron. 14:10, "Is this the right time to attack the Philistines? Will You give me the victory?" God answered him and said, "Attack, and I'll give you the victory." David, in his humility, never assumed anything. He asked God for instructions on what to do. He had won many battles in the past, but still he wanted to hear from God on what to do in this current battle. Generals don't give soldiers the plan for the whole war, just what they have to do next. God has an excellent long-range plan for your life and you need to follow His instructions each and every day. Problems come when you worry about tomorrow instead of doing what you're instructed to do today.

To win the war warriors must always stay at their post. 2 Cor. 6:3,4 (MSG), "People are watching us as we stay at our post, alertly, unswervingly in hard times, tough times, bad times." Warriors go where they're told to go and stay where they're told to stay. If you're a husband and father, stay at your post. Stay home and be the man your family needs you to be. You are called to be a friend to other men so stay at your post. Be by their side when they're going through hard times. Be a friend who sticks closer than a brother (Prov. 18:24). You are a believing warrior, a man of faith, so stay at your post. In the midst of the battle, you need to still believe in the goodness of God, that He will be by your side forevermore. When the enemy surrounds you, when nothing seems to be going your way, worship God and believe you're more than a conqueror and that God always leads you to triumph in Christ (2 Cor. 2:14).

All warriors have a battle cry. Jesus is a warrior and "It is finished!" was His battle cry. David's battle cry against Goliath is found in 1 Sam. 17:45, "I come to you in the name of the Lord of hosts." The power of David was not in his sling; it was in his God. His battle cry is that he came in the strength of the Lord. David then carried the head of Goliath five miles to the enemy-occupied city of Jerusalem (vs. 54).

He was sounding another battle cry. He was saying, "I killed Goliath, and some day I'm coming for you." Whenever the devil attacks you, hold up the head of what you've already defeated. Use what God has already done as a battle cry for what He will do. Say out loud with boldness and confidence, "God delivered me once, He will do it again." Tell the devil, "I've defeated the lion and the bear, and I'll defeat whatever giant you bring against me. No weapon formed against me will prosper." That's your battle cry!

Like all warriors you have a life to live, a dream to fulfill, a race to finish. At the starting line, you're full of hope and excitement but not long after the race begins reality sets in. The race-course is not always easy. There are hills to climb and curves to navigate around. You quickly find out that the race of life isn't pain-free or risk-free. It's a challenge and this is why you have to learn the way of the warrior. One of the most important things every warrior needs is determination. The determination to finish what you start is missing in the lives of most people in the world. They simply don't follow through on what they said they would do. They don't have the determination to seek God until they find Him, to keep working on their marriage, to parent their children through the hard seasons.

God never asks you to do something hard, He asks you to do what is impossible by human standards and this is why faith and determination is always needed. A warrior doesn't mature by how much they know or by how old they are. They mature through what they persevere through. James 1:3 says, "The testing of your faith develops perseverance." Every warrior needs to know it takes perseverance to be determined. Vs. 4, "Perseverance must finish its work so that you may be mature and complete, not lacking anything." You don't persevere in easy times, you only persevere in hard times when you want to quit and walk away. You'll never know all the good that awaits you in the future if you don't persevere in the here and now. Stay in the race. Be determined and persevere especially when quitting would be easier. Determined warriors refuse to back away from their God-assigned path. They fight on until they win.

| 15 |

"LAST MAN STANDING"

Inside of you is the DNA of a warrior, of a man who loves the sting of battle. There is something inside of you that wants to fight, that wants to answer the call to action. Men need to be driven by a cause for which they're willing to fight and die. The call of the warrior is to fight for what they believe in and the cause they want to be a part of. Every warrior knows there are things in life worth fighting for. There are certain values, beliefs, and principles important enough to dedicate oneself to even in the face of adversity. For a warrior to put himself in danger, especially in a life-or-death situation, he must have a good reason for doing so. There must be a cause worth fighting for. When Caleb and eleven others spied out the Promised Land, he was promised a specific mountain once the people of Israel went in and took possession of the land.

Forty-five years later he said to Joshua, "Give me this mountain of which the Lord spoke in that day" (Josh. 14:12). For Caleb, possessing his mountain was a cause worth fighting for. Not only had Caleb served fearlessly as a warrior and spy in his youth, now at the age of eighty-five he still remained full of desire to accomplish the goal set before him. His mountain was full of giants, and he had to drive them out. He was still physically able to do the job but in humility he said, "It may be that the Lord will be with me" (vs. 12). Faith in God is the foundation warriors stand on for it is a strong faith that provides the courage and conviction to address the challenges that come their way. When they face the enemy with faith-filled courage, God steps in and gives them the victory. Always remember, whenever you go to war for God, you are never alone.

Warriors stand up for what is right even if it is difficult or unpopular. They embrace the fight as they actively become engaged in the things that bring glory to God. Caleb exhibited an unquenchable desire to conquer a mountain region that has proven unconquerable well after Joshua led the people into the Promised Land. He wanted that mountain so much that he waited forty-five years to get it. It was the cause he lived for and later would be the cause he would victoriously fight for. Every man needs a cause that fills his heart with passion and fire. History is full of men and women who made an impact on the world because they fought for a cause greater than themselves. Martin Luther King Jr. fought for civil rights and Mother Teresa fought for the poor. Nelson Mandela fought for peace and William Wallace fought for freedom.

A worthy cause will wake you up in the morning as it compels you to go do something with your life that really matters. Never forget that a warrior is only as worthy as his cause. Warriors die daily (1 Cor. 15:31). They die to themselves so they can live for the cause that is bigger than they are. They take up their cross and follow Jesus wherever it may take them (Luke 9:23). Surrender your life to God and He'll give you someone to protect, a kingdom to advance, and a battle to win. Look around you and you'll see there are causes everywhere worth fighting for. Start off by being faithful in the little causes. Take the trash out and do the dishes and iron the clothes. Open the car door for your wife and help get the children ready for bed. He who is faithful over little things will be made ruler over much (Matt. 25:23). There are causes all around you. The danger for many men is they don't have a cause to fight for.

Just before David faced Goliath he was misunderstood and publicly rebuked by his older brother. He said, "What have I done now? Is there not a cause?" (1 Sam. 17:29). David was more concerned with God's cause than with his own feelings. he didn't care about personal glory, he cared only for the glory and success of God's cause. David was clearly a young man on a mission for the cause of God. He knew that a man without a cause becomes passive. He'll be distracted. He'll turn his back on what's important in life. David ruled his emotions and was totally in step with the cause of God Almighty. Goliath was a dead man then and there. This is where the battle was won. This story emphasizes a warrior's sense of duty and his willingness to stand up for what he believes in, to fight on in spite of the ridicule and scorn of others.

He fights because that is what warriors do. God has called every man to be a warrior. Inside of you is the God-given desire to be a mighty man of valor who fights for a godly cause. You were born to fight, and you need to know when to engage in the battle. Men get tired and exhausted when they fight for the wrong things, for things that have no eternal significance. Too many men fight for things that don't matter. They fight for fortune and fame, a new set of golf clubs, a motorcycle, a pool in the back yard, and to be accepted by their peers. What is worth fighting for? Having a close relationship with God and fulfilling your God-given purpose is worth fighting for. A healthy marriage and raising godly children are worth fighting for. Financial freedom and leaving an inheritance to your children's children is worth fighting for. Your physical health, your integrity and character are all things worth fighting for.

Too many men have sat on the sidelines for too long. They have not engaged in the battle God has called them to fight. Because of that, their families have been ripped apart by the enemy. Every warrior knows there can be no victory without sincere faith and strict obedience. Men fail naturally when they fail spiritually, not submitting their will to the will of God. Consider Ps. 78:9,10, "The men of Ephraim, though armed with bows, turned back on the day of battle; they did not keep God's covenant and refused to live by His law." Vs. 32 goes on to say, "In spite of all this, they kept on sinning; in spite of His wonders, they did not believe." They limited a limitless God and failed to walk in victory. The mission of the devil is to steal, kill, and destroy everything that matters to the heart of God (John 10:10). This is why all men need to wake up and prepare for war. They need to step up and protect like a warrior.

How do you protect your family? Eph. 6:11 says, "Put on the whole armor of God that you may be able to stand against the wiles of the devil." Pick up the sword of the Spirit which is the Word of God. Believe God's Word and do what it tells you to do. Choose to be faithful at all times and do those things that are right. Be the spiritual leader your family needs. Be a mighty man of valor in your home. Step up and lead the way. Wake up and prepare for war. Anything worthwhile in life is worth fighting for. Be a warrior and fight back to protect your family from the wiles of the enemy. Love your wife as Christ loves the church and train up your children in the way they should go. The devil can't keep you out of heaven, but he'll sure try to stop you from experiencing heaven on earth today. This is why your mission is to draw near to God and resist the devil at all times (James 4:7).

A warrior is born and bred to fight. He fights and keeps on fighting until he's the last man standing. For sure, there is no second place in a fight to the death. They run their race to win. Every runner knows that as a race progresses, if you don't push yourself harder and harder, you start slowing down and falling back. This is why Paul wrote in 1 Cor. 9:24, "Do you not know that in a race all the runners run, but only one gets the prize? Run in such a way as to get the prize." For the warrior, victory is the only option. 1 Cor. 9:26 (TPT) says, "For this reason, I don't run just for exercise or box like one throwing aimless punches." Run toward the finish line with all you've got and make every blow count. if you throw punches that never hit your opponent then all you're doing is wasting energy.

Be determined to be a winner and make no apology for your desire to win the prize. Don't be like those who take a casual, indifferent attitude toward the Christian life. Seek to run in the light of eternity. Sacrifice everything so that you can follow God without reservation. Invest in the lives of those who minister the Word (Gal. 6:6,7). Minister to those in need (Luke 10:42), give without fanfare (Matt. 6:1), be willing to suffer for the sake of Christ (Matt. 5:11), pray often and in secret (Matt. 6:6). Love your enemies by being willing to help them (Luke 6:35), bless those who cannot repay you (Luke 14:14), give service to the Lord and not just to please men (Col. 3:23). When God is the object of your heart's devotion, and all your energies and talents are used to bring Him glory, nothing will be able to stop you from winning the prize.

Wars are won one battle at a time. The journey you are on may seem to be immeasurably long but remember that you walk a thousand miles one step at a time. The length of your journey is not what's important but rather the direction you are going. God said in Prov. 4:12, "As you go, step by step, I will open up the way before you." Follow God's direction always and He will make your path clear and secure with each step you take. Trust Him even when the finish line is over the horizon. The biggest battles in life are won by patiently continuing to do the right things one small step at a time. J. R. R. Tolkien wrote, "Little by little, one travels far." Understand that the little decisions you make are of infinite importance. They'll cause you to travel great distances with the persistence of moving forward slowly but surely.

In the military a trained foot soldier can travel farther than a horse. Horses must be rested frequently and often die in adverse circumstances. This is why the military equipment and supplies of the Roman army and many others were pulled by oxen and mules which were slower than horses but more persistent. Horse mounted calvary can travel farther in a short time. Although the foot soldier may be slower, by the end of the day he can out travel the horse. Warriors keep moving forward because of their will to persist. James 1:4 says, "Let perseverance finish its work so that you may be mature and complete, not lacking anything." The word "perseverance" also means "patience" or "endurance." Every warrior who fights in a battle knows that patient endurance is how great victories are won."

Warriors in the Lord's army are strong and competent with the ability to act quickly and decisively. They don't hold back when it's time to fight but go to war without hesitation. Battles of any type, physical or spiritual, are lost by hesitation. Those who delay going to war often give the enemy the upper hand in his quest to take you down. Prov. 6:4 (NLT) says, "Don't put it off; do it now! Don't rest until you do." This verse emphasizes the importance of immediate action and not delaying in going to war. Procrastination is "the act of willfully delaying the doing of something that should be done." Sad to say, for some people this is a habitual way of handling any task. The Bible commends hard work (Prov. 12:24) and warns against laziness (Prov. 15:19) and slackness (Prov. 18:9). The cure for procrastination is more diligence regardless of the task.

The warrior should be extremely diligent since it is the Lord's glory he is fighting for. This is why you must put your heart and soul into everything you do for the Lord (Col. 3:23). Never hesitate when the Lord tells you to do something. Everything a warrior does should be characterized by enthusiasm, confidence, and unwavering diligence. He fights and works heartily as unto the Lord. Whatever he does is done with all his might (Eccl. 9:10), in the name of the Lord Jesus (Col. 3:7), to the glory of God (1 Cor. 10:31). When you don't procrastinate you'll be able to make the most of your time and the opportunities God graciously gives you. By using your time effectively you'll move forward and achieve more. Seize the day and don't drive through life with your brakes on. Time is racing by and if you don't act diligently the opportunities you have today may be gone tomorrow.

Life is a battle, and winning is the only option you have. This is why you must win like a warrior. Stand tall and say with confidence, "If God be for us, who can be against us?" The warrior spirit inside of you gives you the determination to take on any challenge, the desire to win at all costs. God is with you and in you and He'll enable you to win the battle you are in. Ex. 14:13 (MSG), "Don't be afraid. Stand firm and watch God do His work of salvation for you today." Warriors fight with everything that is inside of them. They never back down and are never defeated. It is an honor to fight for what is right. If you fight for His cause, you're going to win. Every morning when your feet touch the floor, be prepared for war. Be ready to give all you have. Know the cause you're fighting for. Focus on it. Work for it. Sacrifice for it and confidently fight for it. Fear not because God goes with you and will fight for you against your enemies.

Warriors are not born. They're created through trial and error, pain and suffering, and their ability to conquer their own faults. Warriors grow strong from pain and all the hard times in their life. A warrior's greatest glory is not in never falling, but in rising every time they do fall. Micah 7:8 says, "Do not rejoice over me, my enemy; When I fall, I will arise." If you're in a battle and don't know what to do, be a man and get down on your knees and pray. The strongest man is the one who has faith to believe in God. He is so strong that he can move mountains. The only way to win is to stand with God. Be a man and put your faith and trust in Him. God has never lost a battle and, with Him at your side, neither will you. You are an overcomer! You are more than a conqueror! You can do all things through Christ which gives you strength. Warriors fight! Warriors win! Step up and be the warrior God called you to be.

You are a warrior. Warriors never give up; they don't back down. They pick up their sword and fight. Warriors are disciplined. They are powerful. They are courageous. They are confident. A warrior seeks to act rather than talk. They confront the evil most people refuse to acknowledge. Stand up and roar and let everyone know there is a man in the house. Warriors play a significant role in what happens in their home, their church, their community, and their nation. Stand tall and turn your world upside down. David's mighty men fought to bring honor to their king. We also fight to bring honor to our King, the Lord Jesus Christ. This is why a warrior always gives his best. They go all out in what they do for God. Don't hold back on your commitment to the Lord. Warriors are men of integrity and character who always give more than what is expected of them.

God has given you His absolute best, now you give your absolute best to Him every single day of your life. You will lose the battle and be defeated if all you do is give 95% of your effort. With God, it's all or nothing. Giving less than your best is an offense to God. Men give their best at work so they can get a pay raise. They even give their best on the golf course for the bragging rights it offers. So why give anything but your best to God? Eccl. 9:10 says, "Whatever your hand finds to do, do it with all your might." Rom. 12:11, "Do not let your zeal subside; keep your spiritual fervor, serving the Lord." Give God your best in every area of your life so you'll be completely engaged is everything He is doing. When He is the center of your life, you'll win every battle you fight. Your greatest cause is to live for God totally and completely. Step up and embrace the cause God has called you to. Then fight for it with everything you've got.

| 16 |

"CONTEND FOR THE FAITH"

S ome of the greatest warriors of all time were the Samurai of premodern Japan. The Samurai were elite and highly trained soldiers adept at using both the bow and the sword. The Samurai, or "bushi," were a class of warriors that arose in the 10th century in Japan and performed military service until the 19th century. They were an essential component of Japanese armies in the medieval period. They had high prestige and were given special privileges. All Samurai were supposed to lead their lives according to the ethic "Code of Bushido" which was a philosophy and code of conduct concerning Samurai attitudes, behavior, and lifestyle. The Bushido Code is the code of a warrior. It's the guide for the Samurai in life, battle, and death. It stressed concepts such as loyalty to one's master, self-discipline, and respectful, ethical behavior.

This unique code of principles and morals valued honor, loyalty, compassion, selflessness, and reckless bravery. The values of the Bushido Code are things we can learn from and apply to our everyday lives. A code is something a warrior lives by.

It's what dictates his words and actions all during his life. First and foremost, all warriors were created to give their life away through self-sacrifice. The Samurai is the first to suffer anxiety for human society, and he is the last to seek personal pleasure. The discipline of strength instills resistance without complaint and also teaches courtesy. It demands that we not ruin the pleasure or serenity of others through the expression of our own sadness or pain. We take our own pain so we can help others overcome theirs. Eph. 5:25 says Christ "loved the church and gave Himself for it." As warriors, we must do the same. Exist for the good of others. This will give you a life with purpose, a life of significance.

The sacrifice of Christ on the cross was history's greatest victory. Likewise, the sacrifices you make for the sake of others and the gospel are victories also. When you gave your life to Christ a great sacrifice was made. You died to yourself, and this was indeed a great spiritual triumph for the plan of God. 1 John 3:16 (TPT) says, "Jesus sacrificed His life for us. Because of this great love, we should be willing to lay down our lives for one another." The term "to lay down" means 'to place something in position for a purpose.' It means to do something deliberately, actively, purposefully, and voluntarily. We are called to imitate Jesus in all that we do (1 John 2:6). We are therefore under moral obligation to sacrifice our lives for the advancement of others.

Gary Smalley said, "Surrendering ourselves for others is a regular Christian obligation and should be regarded as an ordinary duty rather than a transcendent deed of virtue." Laying down your life for someone is supreme proof that you love them. John 15:13 says, "Greater love has no one than this, that one lay down his life for his friends." A worthy sacrifice is when you put yourself in harm's way to protect another. This selfless act of heroism mirrors the Lord's sacrifice on the cross. The ultimate act of sacrifice and selfless love is when you deny yourself and put another's life before your own. You give of yourself for another's well-being. A warrior actively serves others with no expectation of receiving anything in return. Caring for others is a visible reflection of the selfless nature of Christian love.

A Samurai knows nothing about surpassing others. They only know how to outdo themselves. As a Samurai, you must strengthen your character. As a human being, you must perfect your spirit. Through intense training and hard work the warrior becomes quick and strong. They develop a power that must be used for good. Inside of him is love and compassion. The true meaning of the term "Samurai" is one who serves and adheres to the power of love. Col. 3:14 says, "But above all these things put on love, which is the bond of perfection." The Phillips Bible says love is "the golden chain of all the virtues." Kenneth Wuest says, "Put on divine and self-sacrificial love which is a binding factor of completeness." Love is the bond of unity for it ties everything together like a belt or a girdle. John MacArthur said love "is the glue that produces unity in the church."

Love is a choice. It's also a matter of conduct. Warriors don't talk about love, they practice it. 1 John 3:18 says, "My little children, let us not love in word or in tongue, but in deed and in truth." There must be corresponding actions to back up everything you say. Don't just talk about love, practice it day by day. Do something about meeting the needs of others. Biblical love is an action. It begins with feelings of concern and compassion for those in need and always results in a tangible, substantial sacrifice. Charles Spurgeon said, "Actions speak louder than words and we shall always be anxious to tell our love in deeds as well as by our lips." This is why warriors go to help others at every opportunity. Nothing is acceptable to God if not motivated by love. Spend your life helping others. The Message Bible says love is "your basic, all-purpose garment. Never be without it."

Warriors are not only respected for their strength in battle but also for their dealings with others. They live to demonstrate love, sympathy, and affection toward those around them. Warriors highlight the importance of valuing and respecting others. They emphasize that true honor goes beyond simply being polite and involves actively elevating others. True warriors have no reason to be cruel. They do not need to prove their strength. Warriors are courteous even to their enemies. For sure, courtesy and good manners will always be noticed. Respect is earned while honor is given freely, often as a gift. Honor involves esteeming others, treating them as if they are valuable and highly treasured. The word "honor" means 'to show high respect for, to count as valuable, to esteem, to honor and revere, to show respect, to recognize one's worth.'

It means 'to fix a value or price upon something or someone and to highly prize it.' The idea is to treat someone as being precious. The person who is honored is elevated above others. Rom. 13:7 (NLT) says, "Give respect and honor to all to whom it is due." Peter said, "Honor all people. Love the brotherhood. Fear God. Honor the king" (1 Peter 2:17). Charles Spurgeon said, "Honor even the poorest of men. Even though they are sunken in vice or crime, honor the manhood that is in them, however much you detest their crimes." He is saying that even though some people are not honorable, honor them anyway just like you are commanded by God to show love to the unlovable. Warriors are commissioned by their Commander-In-Chief to show all men the honor which is due them according to their worth as those made in the image of God.

To master the ways of the Samurai means to have the courage to bear the unbearable. A warrior is worthless unless he rises above his adversaries and stands in the midst of a storm. Sad to say, too many men put up with the harassments of the enemy without putting up a fight to see those circumstances changed for the better. Jesus survived the unthinkable in the Garden of Gethsemane when He said, "My soul is very sorrowful, even to death; remain here and watch with Me" (Matt. 36:38). For Jesus, the agony of the cross had begun. Anguish pressed in on Him until His "sweat became like great drops of blood falling to the ground" (Luke 22:44). What Jesus did in His suffering teaches us how we also can bear the unbearable. The first thing He did was "He fell on His face and prayed" (Matt. 26:39).

Prayer doesn't change God's plans; it brings your heart and your plans into alignment with His. When the unbearable comes upon you, humbly fall before God in full surrender and pray. Next, you must die to your own will. Jesus said, "My Father, if it be possible, let this cup pass from Me; nevertheless, not My will, but Your will be done" (Matt. 26:39). Jesus died to His own will because He fully trusted the will of the Father. Depend on the indwelling power of the Holy Spirit and wholeheartedly embrace the will of God. After you've prayed and released your will, stand up and face the challenge before you. Jesus said to His disciples, "Rise, let us be going; see, My betrayer is at hand" (Matt. 25:46). Once you've embraced God's will, get up and get going knowing that God will never leave you or forsake you (Heb. 13:5). Keep your eyes on His faithfulness and move forward.

Hiding like a turtle in a shell is not living. All men need to stir up the warrior within and break into the life God intends for them to have. Everyone feels fear. The question is, what do you do when you feel fear? Teddy Roosevelt said, "Courage is not having the strength to go on; it's going on when you don't have the strength." Yes, sometimes we'll fall, break, and fail. But then we rise up. We heal. We overcome. An ancient Jewish proverb says, "I ask not for a lighter burden, but for broader shoulders." Admiral James Stockdale said, "You must retain faith that you will prevail in the end, regardless of the difficulties. At the same time, you must confront the most brutal facts of your current reality, whatever they may be." Jude 3 says, "I found it necessary to write to you exhorting you to contend earnestly for the faith." In the war between good and evil you must fight with intensity and great determination.

The battles we fight are a matter of life and death. This is why the Message Bible says, "I have to write insisting - begging! - that you fight with everything you have in you for this faith." You never fight your battles from a rocking chair or a soft bed. This is a strenuous struggle where you expend all your energy in order to prevail. Just as the Greek athletes exerted themselves to the point of agony in an effort to win the contest, so do the warriors of God exert intense effort in the battles they fight. No longer are we to settle for the devil's constant attacks, for perpetual sickness, for a life of mediocrity. Warriors are not called to a life of complacency. They are called to contend for the faith. The word "contend" means 'to struggle in prevailing over opposition.' A true warrior must have heroic courage. The Samurai always has to rise and move on because new challenges will come.

Yes, life is a struggle but the greater the difficulty, the more glory in overcoming it. Skillful pilots gain their reputation from storms and tempests. Be grateful for adversity for it forces the human spirit to grow. No pain, no gain. Surely, human character is formed not in the absence of difficulty but in our response to it. Scripture commands all men to stand up, be strong, and do battle against the flesh and the devil. To do that, you must get fed up with being held down and harassed by the enemy. Rise up and fight the good fight of faith. Refuse to live deprived, joyless, and empty lives. Stop living in dark caves and cold dens where you are scared and feel helpless all the time. Once and for all get thoroughly disgusted. Tell the devil, "This has gone far enough! I serve a mighty and victorious God, and I will no longer take your abuse!"

Losers quit and run away while winners show up and keep showing up. They say, "The Lord is my strength and my shield; My heart trusted in Him, and I am helped" (Ps. 28:7). The moment you stop fighting and contending for the faith is when you'll slide into a state of complacency and give the devil the upper hand over your life. Complacency and the life of a warrior are completely incompatible. It's like oil and water. They don't mix. If you don't stand up and fight, you'll inevitably start heading downstream with everybody else. Many men today are bullied by the enemy because the warrior spirit within is dormant. They put up with financial hardship, sickness and disease, and strife and division in their relationships. There comes a time, however, when you can take only so much of the enemy's attacks on a constant basis. The warrior spirit is there but it's asleep and needs to be awakened.

You never know how strong you are until being strong is the only choice you have. The most significant and successful warrior is the man who has gone through insurmountable trials. John Bunyan said, "I have often thought that the best Christians are found in the worst of times." Are you tired of the devil harassing you? Then wake up and prepare for war! Draw a line in the sand and say, "No more! Enough is enough! Today I fight!" One of the first things God wants to teach you is how to fight for all men are born into a war. Jesus said, "The kingdom of heaven suffers violence, and the violent take it by force" (Matt. 11:12). The TPT says, "Passionate people have taken hold of its power." The kingdom of God is both advancing and being attacked. Seeking first the advancement of

God's kingdom takes earnest endeavor, untiring energy, and utmost exertion.

Violence is brought against the kingdom of God by those outside of it. Men of valor are eager for the glories of the kingdom of heaven, and they must also fight violently to defend it. Faith and holy violence are inseparably connected. Possession comes by force. Faith is a living power from heaven which grasps and takes by force the promises God has given. Men who complain they've never received the blessings of God probably haven't been violent about it. They think if they only persevere everything will be okay. No! You must wake up and prepare for war. You must fight violently against the forces of darkness in order to receive all that Jesus died to give you. You need to accept the fact that warfare is the lifestyle of every man in the kingdom of God. All warriors are engaged in a constant battle. If you don't defeat the enemy, he will surely defeat you.

Mighty men do mighty works for the Lord God Almighty. This is the purpose for which they were born. This is the destiny they strive every day to fulfill. When you maximize the manhood in a man, the power of God will flow through his life and into the world around him. The result of this is that the world will be made a better place. Mighty men are not moved by the culture today that is trying to snuff out the power God has given man to rule and reign on the earth. They rise up and go forward. The question is, are you doing what a mighty man of God should do? Are you leading your wife or is she leading you? Do you fight or do you run away? Mighty men are created in the likeness and image of God. He didn't create you to be ordinary, He created you to be mighty, to be used for His glory and honor.

A mighty man is God-filled, God-inspired, God-anointed, and God-empowered. He's made in the image of God and boldly he marches into battle. You are here to bring a positive change to your home, your church, your community, your nation, and all over the world. You are here to be a mighty man of God. You are here to declare that Jesus is the King of kings and Lord of lords, the great "I AM." By your words and actions you reveal to people the love and character of God. A mighty man is not satisfied with marginal responsibility but rather wants the will of God to be fulfilled in his life fully and completely. There is no limit to what He will do for his Heavenly Father. When God wants something done a mighty man will step forward without hesitation and with great eagerness say, "Here I am! Send me!" (Is. 6:8). That's the way of a warrior.

SUMMARY

The call to every man is urgent and unmistakable: to rise and fulfill the role God has assigned as a warrior in His kingdom. As Joel 3:9–10 proclaims, God commands His people to prepare for battle, to sharpen their strength, and to take their stand against the forces of injustice and evil. These battles are not always fought with swords or shields, but with courage, faith, and unwavering obedience to His Word. Each man is called to train his spirit, discipline his heart, and commit himself fully to the work God has entrusted to him.

Being a warrior in the kingdom of God is not about pride, aggression, or worldly power - it is about readiness, integrity, and dedication to God's purposes. It is about standing firm when the world wavers, speaking truth when lies abound, and defending righteousness even in the face of opposition. Every act of obedience, every step of faith, and every moment of courage strengthens not only the individual but also advances the kingdom of God on earth.

Men of God, the time has come to awaken! The battle is real, the call is urgent, and the kingdom of God is advancing. Now is the time to rise as warriors, to be equipped, disciplined, and ready to fight for righteousness. This is not a fight for fame, comfort, or personal gain. It is a fight for truth, justice, and the glory of God. Every man is entrusted with a mission to stand firm when others falter, to speak boldly when lies surround, and to act courageously when fear whispers.

The battles you face may not always be seen by the world, but they are no less real in the spiritual realm. Each act of faith, each decision to obey God, and each step into courage becomes a weapon in His hands. Do not shrink back. Do not grow weary. Prepare your heart, sharpen your spirit, and put on the full armor of God. The kingdom needs warriors who will rise above weakness, stand against compromise, and march forward with unwavering devotion. God calls you not because you are strong, but because He is mighty and His strength will carry you through every battle.

This book has sought to awaken the warrior within, to challenge men to embrace their calling, and to provide the guidance necessary to prepare for the battles that lie ahead. Let these pages serve as a reminder that God's army is not made up of the strongest or the most experienced, but of those who are willing to be used, equipped, and empowered by Him. Prepare, therefore, with diligence. Stand, therefore, with courage. Fight, therefore, with faith. The kingdom of God is advancing, and the time for action is now. Step into your calling. Stand in your purpose. Fight with faith.